For my father

THE RIGHT REVEREND ALEXANDER D. STEWART, Episcopal bishop of Western Massachusetts, says:

"Coming at this time, Howe's book fulfills a vital need. No longer will conflict within the Episcopal church be between parties in churchmanship or liturgy. . . . The persistent conflict will be between Anglicans who wish to preserve the biblical roots of their apostolic tradition and those who would endorse the latest theological fad and thus minimize the biblical basis of our faith.

". . . Anglicans who cherish our emphasis on Scripture, tradition, and reason will recognize these three strands woven together here. John Howe recognizes that Anglicans' minds are not made on a Xerox machine and that 'My answer may not be your answer.'

"But great Anglicans have always recognized that while they may differ in their interpretation of God's acts or of Christ's words, God did act and Christ did leave us some specific commands.

"*Our Anglican Heritage* will help you appreciate the glories of Anglicanism at its best . . ."

–*from the foreword*

OUR ANGLICAN HERITAGE

JOHN W. HOWE

David C. Cook Publishing Co.

ELGIN, ILLINOIS—WESTON, ONTARIO
FULLERTON, CALIFORNIA

Acknowledgments
I would like to express my gratitude
to the Reverend Doctors Philip E. Hughes,
John H. Rodgers, Jr.,
John R. W. Stott, and Duane H. Thebeau
for reading various portions of the manuscript
and making many helpful suggestions regarding it.

Published by David C. Cook Publishing Co., Elgin, IL 60120
Printed in the United States of America

Library of Congress Catalog Number: 77-78492
ISBN: 0-89191-079-4

All the major elements of the Reformation were in Wyclif: the revolt against the worldliness of the clergy, and the call for a sterner morality; the return from the Church to the Bible, from Aquinas to Augustine, from free will to predestination, from salvation by works to election by divine grace; the rejection of indulgences, auricular confession, and transubstantiation; the deposition of the priest as an intermediary between God and man; the protest against the alienation of national wealth to Rome; the invitation to the state to end its subordination to the papacy; the attack (preparing for Henry VIII) on the temporal possessions of the clergy. If the Great Revolt had not ended the government's protection of Wyclif's efforts, the Reformation might have taken form and root in England 130 years before it broke out in Germany.

Will Durant
The Reformation
(The Story of Civilization, Volume VI)

CONTENTS

FOREWORD

The task of describing our entire Anglican heritage could produce either a multivolume work that no one would finish or else a synopsis so slight that the reader would receive only hors d'oeuvres, not a satisfying meal. With the gift of the artist and the skill of the teacher, John Howe conveys profundity with simplicity and brevity.

While emphasizing the biblical basis of authority stressed by the Anglican church, Howe yet echoes Phillips Brooks' phrase that we are "the roomiest church in Christendom."

He does not gloss over or treat lightly those embarrassing incidents, those stupid blunders, those uncharitable moments in our history. Thus he is true to biblical tradition, which records both the errors and accomplishments of good men.

This is a worthy successor to those books of

yesteryear—*The Episcopal Church* by the memorable Dean Hodges, *The Episcopal Church: Its Message for Men of Today* by Atwater, and *The Episcopal Church and Its Work* from the popular teaching series of the 1950s.

In reading this book, one remembers fondly the writings of the late Bishop Angus Dun on the Episcopal church and the creeds. Some recent books of this sort have had a breezy, popular approach but lacked Howe's scholarship and comprehensiveness.

Coming at this time, Howe's book fulfills a vital need. No longer will conflict within the Episcopal church be between parties in churchmanship or liturgy. In time even the controversy on women's ordination will cease to be at the forefront.

The persistent conflict will be between Anglicans who wish to preserve the biblical roots of the apostolic tradition and those who would endorse the latest theological fad (which come and go these days in three-year cycles) and thus minimize the biblical basis of our faith.

Not all Episcopalians will like this book, especially those whose current theology is based on Marxian premises (though they may not realize this) or in doctrines of human behavior that are at variance with the classical Christian doctrine of man.

However, the great Anglicans who cherish our emphasis on Scripture, tradition, and reason will recognize these three strands woven together here. John Howe recognizes that Anglicans' minds are not made on a Xerox machine and that "My answer may not be your answer." Nor have we in the Anglican tradition ever welcomed an IBM programming of our liturgy or our lives.

But great Anglicans have always recognized that, while they may differ in their interpretation of God's acts or of Christ's words, God did act and Christ did leave us some specific commands. This was expressed by Queen Elizabeth I during an early controversy about the Lord's Supper,

> 'Twas God the Word that spake it,
> He took the Bread and brake it;
> And what the Word did make it;
> That I believe, and take it.

Our Anglican Heritage will help you appreciate the glories of Anglicanism at its best and the Episcopal church's essential role as the bridge church in ecumenical dialogue between the Reformation tradition and the church Catholic. Both of these traditions are now achieving that balance of word and sacrament so prized in the apostolic era. Those Christians coming from the Reformation tradition have gained a new appreciation of the sacraments, while our brothers and sisters from the Catholic traditions have joyously discovered the richness of Holy Scripture.

Hence we see emerging the balance so aptly phrased by Saint Luke when he described the followers of the way. "And they continued stedfastly in the apostles' doctrine and fellowship, and in the breaking of bread, and in prayers'' (Acts 2:42, KJV). As Anglicans, our spiritual parentage is clearly rooted in the Scriptures and the sacraments. So may it continue by God's grace.

THE RIGHT REVEREND ALEXANDER D. STEWART
Episcopal Bishop of Western Massachusetts

1

The Break with Rome:
the Mixing of Politics and Religion

No, THE CHURCH OF ENGLAND did *not* begin in the sixteenth century. It was *not* founded by Henry VIII. It was *not* simply a matter of his wanting a divorce so he could marry Anne Boleyn. But these are some of the widely held misconceptions, even among Anglicans themselves.

The Church of England has a rich biblical and theological heritage. Its reformation was as much a protest against Roman Catholic heresy as were the Lutheran and Calvinist movements on the Continent. In this case, however, the break with Rome mixed politics with religion.

When was the Christian gospel first proclaimed in Britain? No one knows for sure. English folklore has it that Saint Paul, Joseph of Arimathea, and even

Jesus himself visited the British Isles during the dawning days of Christian history.

> And did those feet, in ancient times,
> Walk upon England's mountains green?
> And was the holy Lamb of God
> On England's pleasant pastures seen?

—William Blake

A more accurate answer, perhaps, is that Roman soldiers or British merchants with dealings in the Holy Land brought back the message of the God who became man. We do know that long before the Nicene Creed was adopted as the expression of Catholic faith (A.D. 325), a vigorous Christianity had sprung up throughout southern Britain and that three English bishops attended the first meeting of Christian bishops in the Western Roman Empire, the Synod of Arles in 314. By the time Augustine arrived from Rome to become the first archbishop of Canterbury in 597, Celtic Christians, as they were called, were already sending their own missionaries—soon to go as far afield as Germany and Switzerland.

British allegiance to Roman Catholicism was not formalized until the Synod of Whitby in the seventh century, and by then many local customs and emphases were firmly established in English faith and practice. The early kings, for instance, retained

16

their own right to approve all ecclesiastical appointments and forbade the removal of English court cases to Rome. A certain tension between conformity and independence characterized English Christianity almost from the beginning.

By the fourteenth century, Roman Catholicism had evolved into something very different from the "faith once delivered to the saints." The Bible had been interpreted and reinterpreted by various church councils and finally forced into categories of Aristotelian philosophy by Thomas Aquinas. Salvation was no longer a matter of simply trusting God's graciousness, but increasingly, it was seen as something we earn. In the popular mind, forgiveness could be bought and sold through a system of indulgences. The communion meal had become an elaborate sacrifice, offered on an altar by a priest in whose hands the bread and wine were to be literally transformed into Christ's body and blood. The pope claimed political as well as religious supremacy and financed his wars through taxation of the faithful. Of course, the Mass was in Latin and was only poorly understood by most of the clergy, not at all by the ordinary Christian.*

One of the clearest voices calling for reform was that of John Wycliffe, an Englishman. In open defiance of Rome, Wycliffe (1320?-1384) translated

---

*Hocus pocus derives from *hoc es corpus meum,* Latin for "This is my body."

the major portion of the Bible into English and called for the church to return to the Scriptures. The principle of *sola Scriptura* ("the Scriptures only"), which became the battle cry of the Reformation, was trumpeted in England a century and a half before Luther nailed his ninety-five theses to the door of the Wittenberg church. Wycliffe himself was silenced, but his followers, the Lollards, persisted. As Bishop Stephen Neill writes, "It is not surprising that the Reformers believed themselves to be reaping where Wyclif had sown."[1]

At least three other major factors paved the way for the break with Rome. First, there was the impact of the Renaissance and its critical undermining of papal authority. It was clearly proven that many of the most important apostolic and later documents on which the pope's authority was based were outright forgeries from as late as the ninth century. If the basis for claiming dominion was false, what status could the claim itself have?

Secondly, propaganda: the power of the printing press made possible what was never before imagined—the wholesale distribution of tracts and pamphlets as well as the Scriptures in the language of the common man. This was Luther's greatest tool. His books were distributed throughout Europe, and by the early 1520s, the Lutheran movement was well established in Cambridge. Groups of young theologians and clergy gathered at the White Horse Tavern to discuss Luther's works and were dubbed "the

Germans.'' By the time Henry VIII declared his independence from Rome, perhaps 50 percent of the English bishops were of Lutheran persuasion.

Thirdly, there was a rising tide of nationalism, a desire on the part of both church and state to limit the interference of any foreign power—including the pope—in the internal affairs of the realm. The conviction that England should be English lay at the root of Henry's political support.

Henry's immediate problem was the need to dissolve his marriage. His queen, Catherine of Aragon, had been married to his older brother Arthur in 1501 (when Arthur was fourteen, Catherine sixteen). But Arthur died within six months, and the marriage was never consummated. Henry VII then had Catherine married to his younger son, Henry VIII, then only ten years old! This was contrary to canon law, but Pope Julius II granted a dispensation. Henry fathered six children by Catherine, but only Mary survived infancy.

In the year 1525 Queen Catherine turned forty, and Henry was still without a legitimate male heir. A woman had never ruled England, and it was an open question whether one could. The only previous experience was the disastrous attempt of Matilda, which brought on the Wars of Succession. As Roland Bainton puts it, ''The problem . . . was not passion but succession. [Henry] knew how to satisfy passion without benefit of matrimony.''[2]

Henry argued that the dispensation should never

19

have been granted. Royal childlessness (disregarding Mary) was a fulfillment of the Levitical curse: "If a man shall take his brother's wife, it is an unclean thing . . . they shall be childless" (Lev. 20:21, KJV). Henry petitioned Pope Clement VII to set aside the dispensation and annul the marriage.

But then the plot thickened. In 1527 Charles V of Spain, emperor of the Holy Roman Empire, sacked Rome. The pope became a prisoner of the emperor and remained under his domination even when released. And Queen Catherine of England was Charles's aunt!

Henry couldn't legitimize an heir without an annulment from the pope; the pope couldn't grant an annulment without offending the emperor; and the emperor couldn't extend his approval without damaging the reputation of his aunt. In short, the national interests of England were dictated via the papacy by the government of Spain.

The pope delayed and equivocated. At one point he even suggested that, under the circumstances, it might be permissible for Henry to commit bigamy. By 1529 it was clear he would not act. In the meantime Henry had fallen in love with Anne Boleyn and decided to take things into his own hands.

He began by intimidating the clergy, charging that they had illegally recognized Thomas Wolsey as papal legate, though he had also. He forbade the passage of church laws without his consent and curtailed the payment of taxes to the pope. He forced the adoption of a declaration that he was "single and supreme Lord, and, as far as the law of Christ allows, even supreme head" of the Church of England. He selected Thomas Cranmer as the new archbishop of Canterbury, largely because Cranmer sided with him. Finally, he persuaded Parliament to forbid the clergy any appeal to Rome and require that they continue their ministerial functions despite the breach that was obviously imminent. The stage was set.

In 1534, on authority of Parliament and the archbishop of Canterbury, the Act of Succession declared the marriage of Henry and Catherine null and void. (He had already married Anne just in time to legitimize the birth of their child: the future Queen Elizabeth—a girl after all!)

In November, 1534, the Act of Supremacy declared: "The king's majesty justly and rightly is and ought to be and shall be reputed the only supreme head in earth of the Church of England called *Anglicana Ecclesia*." Leaving spiritual functions such as administering the sacraments to the clergy, he had, in effect, replaced the pope with the king. The church remained Catholic, but the break with Rome was complete.

* * *

How shall we view such maneuverings? Scripture abounds with tales of men and women pursuing their own various goals who find themselves thrust, inadvertently, onto the center stage of God's unfolding drama. Joseph's brothers sold him into Egyptian slavery, only to find years later that he alone could rescue them from starvation. Behind their sinfulness, Joseph recognized the gracious hand of God: "It was not you who sent me here, but God" (Gen. 45:8).

David committed adultery and murder to satisfy his lust for Bathsheba, but that very union established the royal lineage that led to Christ.

Augustus Caesar demanded a census for the purpose of taxation, and it forced a certain couple to make a very difficult journey to a town called Bethlehem. Thus Scripture was fulfilled (Mic. 5:2), and God's Word became flesh.

Henry was no noble king. His purposes were far from godly. Some of the bishops and theologians who helped him compromised at several points. Yet, there can be no doubt that in the midst of all the power politics, all the intrigue and rationalization, and all the compromise and outright sin on both sides, *God was returning the Church of England to its biblical foundations*.

Even under Henry's basically Catholic rule, two major changes were introduced with far-reaching consequences. First, the Bible was again translated into English (by William Tyndale and later by Miles Coverdale), and copies were introduced into all the churches in England. People crowded into them all day long, simply to hear the Scriptures read.

Secondly, the genius of Archbishop Cranmer began to shine in the area of worship. Convinced that prayer should be in the language of the people, he began to fashion what has come to be known as *The Book of Common Prayer*. Beginning with the Litany and coming at last to the full-scale prayer books of 1549 and 1552, Cranmer bequeathed to the English-speaking world a form of worship so majestic as to be without rival. The fact that the majority of his phrases came down to the present generation virtually unchanged speaks for itself. It has been said that perhaps no other writer except Tennyson had as acute a sensitivity to the exact sound and impact of every English vowel, the cadence of every consonant. Cranmer gave worship back to the people, and he did so magnificently.

Eventually, he fashioned a lectionary (a daily and weekly schedule of Bible readings), and in a stroke he made the Church of England the greatest Bible-reading church in the world. Nowhere else is the Bible read so regularly, so comprehensively, and at such length as in the public worship of the Anglican communion.

In 1547 King Henry died, and Edward VI, son of the third of his scandalous series of marriages, came to the throne at age nine. The Boy King ruled, under two protectorates, a mere six years before succumbing to his always frail health. But what massive changes took place during those years!

The Roman Mass was transformed into a Com-

munion meal once again. Wine, previously reserved
for the clergy, was distributed along with the bread
to all communicants. The bread itself was real bread
instead of a special wafer. The altar was replaced by
the Holy Table. By law it had to be made of wood
and moved away from the wall into the middle of the
congregation. Adoration of the communion elements (and anything that hinted of it) was prohibited.
The prayer of transubstantiation, that the bread and
wine become Christ's body and blood, was elimi-
nated. The words of distribution were reduced to
simply "Take and eat this" or "Drink this in remembrance." Ritual gestures were forbidden. So
were prayers for the dead and every reference to
purgatory. The priest's vestments were reduced to
cassock and surplice (a black robe with a simple
white overrobe). Clergy were freely permitted to
marry.

In the midst of all these specifics, the central point
of difference between the Church of England and the
Church of Rome emerged. In 1545 the pope con-
vened the Council of Trent. It declared what had
long been practice: that regarding authority, Roman
Catholicism gives equal veneration to the Scriptures
and the traditions of the church, written and unwritten.

In the sharpest contrast, Anglicanism stands for
what Bishop Neill calls the "position held by the
Church through the centuries"—the ultimate authority of Scripture alone (sola Scriptura). "From this

24

standard," he says, "the Church of Rome has departed, with disastrous consequences to herself." By her compromise, she is simply "not the great historic Church of the West."[3]

Questions for Thought and Discussion

1. What is the most important difference between the Anglican church and the Roman Catholic church?

2. What was the relationship between the Reformation in England and on the Continent at this time?

3. Were the reasons for separating from the Catholic church sound? Do some remnants of the beliefs and ritual of the Catholic church remain today?

4. What were the changes introduced during the reign of Edward VI and how do they relate to the Episcopal church today? Do you agree with these changes?

5. Can you think of contemporary examples of God's involvement in political affairs? Is it possible to tell?

2

The Counter-Reformation:
Bloody Mary's Return to Rome

EDWARD VI DIED in 1553, and following a brief political struggle, the succession King Henry had tried to prevent became a reality: Mary Tudor ascended the throne of England. For Mary it had been a bitter twenty years since the annulment of her mother's marriage and the declaration that she was illegitimate. During all that time, she had remained unswervingly devoted to Roman Catholicism, though her life was often endangered by her dedication. Now, she felt God had chosen her to restore the Roman faith to England.

Her weapon was persecution. During the five years of her reign, nearly three hundred "heretics" were burned alive, and countless others starved to death in English prisons. It was, of course, a time of persecution. Historians have sometimes minimized Mary's violence by pointing out that even "the good

Queen Elizabeth'' sent dissenters to their death. **But** the similarity must not be exaggerated. Under **both** Elizabeth and Henry, only those considered distinctly subversive to the government were executed. But under Mary, to quote Bishop J. C. Ryle, the martyrs ''were not rebels against the Queen's authority, caught redhanded in arms. They were not thieves, or murderers, or drunkards, or unbelievers, or men and women of immoral lives. On the contrary, they were, with barely an exception, some of the holiest, purest, and best Christians in England, and several of them the most learned men of their day.''[4]

Certainly from a numerical point of view alone, there has never been, before or since, an English sovereign who so deserved the epithet ''Bloody'' as did Queen Mary Tudor. Among the martyrs were fifty-five women, four children, about a hundred priests, four bishops, and the archbishop of Canterbury. It was a dark and terrible time for England, and for Christendom.

But, as Tertullian had said of the early apostles, ''The blood of the martyrs is the seed of the Church.'' Mary had hoped to reestablish Roman Catholicism throughout the land. She achieved exactly the opposite: her persecutions guaranteed the success of the Reformation. And, in the process she exacted some of the noblest expressions of biblical faith the world has seen.

What may be difficult to grasp is the fact that the

whole persecution turned on a single theological issue: *the doctrine of the real presence.*

The Roman Catholic church had come to teach that the body and blood of Christ were literally and materially present in the bread and wine of the Mass. This was the miracle of *transubstantiation.* The bread still looked, felt, smelled, and tasted like bread. But its substance—what it *really* was beneath these appearances—was transformed into Christ's body. The wine still appeared to be wine, but it too was miraculously transformed into Christ's blood. The sacrifice was thus offered anew at every Mass. Here atonement for sin was made. Here God's grace was dispensed. To share in the Mass was to be included in forgiveness; to miss it was to be excluded. Thus the Mass was and is indispensable to the whole system of Roman Catholic theology. And the doctrine of the real presence was and is at the heart of the Protestant controversy.

Did one believe this or not? If he did, all else could be tolerated. If not, he faced the stake and flames.

Does it seem just so much argument over words? Is it incredible that men should have died rather than agree to such a doctrine? More incredible still that others should have demanded their deaths?

In his remarkable little book, *Five English Reformers,* Bishop J. C. Ryle demonstrates that in this seemingly innocuous question the whole Christian gospel is at stake. Ryle contends that if one grants that the bread and wine are the body and blood of Christ and that the Lord's Supper is a sacrifice, not a sacrament, then

> you spoil the blessed doctrine of *Christ's finished work* when he died on the cross. A sacrifice that needs to be repeated is not a perfect and complete thing. You spoil the *priestly office* of Christ. If there are priests that can offer an acceptable sacrifice to God besides him, the great High Priest is robbed of his glory. You spoil the Scriptural doctrine of the *Christian ministry*. You exalt sinful men into the position of mediators between God and man. You give to the sacramental elements of bread and wine an honor and veneration they were never meant to receive, and produce an *idolatry* to be abhorred of faithful Christians. Last, but not least, you overthrow the true doctrine of *Christ's human nature*. If the body born of the Virgin Mary can be in more places than one at the same time, it is not a body like our own, and Jesus was not "the second Adam" in the truth of our nature.[5]

There were subsidiary matters. Some were attacked for their teaching regarding the nature of the church, or the marriage of priests, or some other such issue. But it was clearly and without exception the doctrine of the real presence that marked men for life or death.

The first victim of Mary's persecution was John Rogers, a clergyman attached to Saint Paul's Cathedral, burned at the stake in London on February 4, 1555. When the lord chancellor asked Rogers if he believed the sacrament was the very body and blood of Christ, really and substantially, Rogers replied emphatically no. "For I cannot understand the words *really* and *substantially* to signify otherwise than corporally: but corporally Christ is only in heaven."[6]

For this great crime, Rogers was held under house arrest for over half a year, then confined at Newgate prison for a full year—the whole time without any support for himself or his wife and ten children. Finally, when he would not recant, he was burned.

Before the end of the year over seventy-five others had joined him, most notably the former bishops Ridley and Latimer.[7] Prior to the end of 1553, these two bishops had been confined to the Tower of London, along with Archbishop Cranmer. Later, they were transferred to the Bocardo at Oxford, which Bishop Coverdale described as "a stinking and filthy prison for drunkards, whores and harlots, and the vilest sort of people." Having inherited leadership in the church when most of the clergy knew nothing of the Bible and some could not even repeat the Lord's Prayer, they had not only helped rediscover the gospel; they reinstituted preaching. Latimer, in particular, aroused hundreds of his listeners to search the Scriptures and know their saving truths.

The revival of faith they helped to lead was also a revival of charity. Ridley, Latimer, and most of the other leaders who perished under Mary set new stan-

30

dards for visiting and caring for the poor, the sick, the widows, the orphans, and those in prison. These were scholars of excellence, but they majored in people. They were known and loved throughout the realm. But when Mary's anger was unleashed against the Reformation, their end came quickly.

They were taken to the north side of Oxford and required to listen to a sermon denouncing them and their doctrine. Ridley begged the vice chancellor an opportunity to reply. "Mr. Ridley," he said, "if you will revoke your erroneous opinions, you shall not only have liberty so to do, but also your life."

"Not otherwise?" asked Ridley.

"No," he was told. "If you will not do so, there is no remedy; you must suffer for your deserts."

"Well," said Ridley, "so long as the breath is in my body, I will never deny my Lord Christ and his known truth. God's will be done in me." Then, in a loud voice, "I commit our cause to Almighty God, who will indifferently judge all."

Latimer added, "There is nothing hid but it shall be opened."

They were commanded to prepare for the stake. Having already given away all their worldly belongings, they were now stripped to their undergarments and chained to a post. A bag of gunpowder was tied about each of their necks, and the wood was lighted. Then Latimer spoke his final words: *"Be of good comfort, Mr. Ridley, and play the man! We shall this day light such a candle, by God's grace, in England, as I trust never shall be put out."*

Watching the double burning from his prison window, Cranmer knew his own ordeal was just ahead. In some ways, it was to be the most difficult of all. Cranmer was the most influential of the Reformers and was probably the most sensitive as well. Having begun a loyal Catholic, with reservations only on England's political independence, his theology had become thoroughly Reformed. He had even offered to prove in public debate that "all the doctrine and religion set forth by our Sovereign Lord King Edward the Sixth is more pure and according to God's Word than any other that hath been used in England these thousand years."[8]

But Cranmer was still a political creature. And politically, he faced a dilemma. Having broken with Rome out of allegiance to the crown, what was he to do now that the crown had returned to Rome?

Cranmer wavered, and finally, after intense pressure, he recanted. It was a sorry fall; the news was trumpeted throughout the land. But his persecutors were not satisfied. They were determined to humiliate the whole Reformation in the person of Archbishop Cranmer, and they demanded his death.

Having signed several documents of recantation already, Cranmer was ordered to repudiate the Reformation in public before facing the stake ("that . . . all men may understand that you are a Catholic indeed"[9]). But Cranmer turned his degradation into glory.

He began by voicing his sorrow at having embraced so wrong a cause. But his true meaning was hidden: the wrong cause was not the Reformation, but his denial of it! Archbishop Marcus Loane writes, "he managed his speech with such skill that he was allowed to run on at some length before its real drift was perceived."[10] Finally it was evident:

" 'And now,' he said, 'I come to the great thing that troubleth my conscience more than any other thing that ever I said or did in my life, and that is the setting abroad of writings contrary to the truth: which here now I renounce and refuse . . . .

" 'And forasmuch as my hand offended in writing contrary to my heart, therefore my hand shall first be punished; for if I may come to the fire, it shall first be burned.

" 'As for the Pope, I refuse him as Christ's enemy and anti-Christ, with all his false doctrine. And as for the sacrament—'

"He could get no further; all the pent-up fury of a thunderstruck audience broke out."[11] He was dragged from the stage and hurried toward the stake. But he himself set the pace, striding so quickly that the friars accompanying him had to run to keep up.

And then, as the fire leapt up, he held the offending hand in the flames until it burned to a stump, crying, "Lord Jesus, receive my spirit."

* * *

One can hardly help remembering that sturdy

apostle who promised to go with Jesus to the death but denied him three times before the cock crowed the next day. On the beach one morning after the resurrection, Jesus promised that same apostle that by his own death he would glorify God (John 21:19). Peter was later to write, "Beloved, do not be surprised at the fiery ordeal which comes upon you . . . after you have suffered a little while, the God of all grace, who has called you to his eternal glory in Christ, will himself restore, establish, and strengthen you. To him be the dominion for ever and ever. Amen" (I Peter 4:12; 5:10, 11).

Queen Mary's own death came on November 17, 1558. It is quite certain that the martyrdoms during her reign did more to spread the sentiment for reformation than all previous governmental efforts.

Questions for Thought and Discussion

1. What effect did Mary Tudor's return to the Catholic church and her subsequent persecution have on the Reformation in England?

2. Why was the doctrine of the real presence a central issue in Mary's persecution?

3. What effect does belief in the real presence and transubstantiation have on the Communion service? On the priesthood of Christ?

4. Do you agree with Bishop Ryle that accepting the doctrine of the real presence and transubstantia-

tion is untrue to the concept of Christ as portrayed in the Bible? Is this doctrine a crucial theological issue?

5. Are there Episcopalians today who believe in the real presence and transubstantiation?

6. Are there places in the world today where Christians are suffering for their faith? Someone has asked, ''If Christians were being killed for their faith in this country, would there be enough evidence to convict you?'' Would there? Would you die for a theological belief?

3

The Elizabethan Settlement:
the Bridge Church

IT HAS BEEN SAID that Elizabeth had no genuine religious convictions, that her decisions were entirely political. If so, she had remarkable insight as to what would make for stability in a kingdom that had been Catholic, Protestant, then Catholic again in less than a quarter of a century. Mary Tudor had been pronounced illegitimate by the Protestants; Elizabeth was declared so by the Catholics. Like her half-sister, she had known a terrifying childhood. Elizabeth had seen the folly and tragedy of imposing a narrow sectarianism through persecution. Whether from conviction or out of sheer pragmatics, Elizabeth sought a broad comprehensiveness within the basic Protestantism that survived her sister's reign of terror.

Within a few months of her accession to the throne, Parliament passed a new Supremacy Act, rejecting again the authority of the pope and all payments and appeals to him. There was, however, at Elizabeth's own insistence, a significant change of title. Instead of being called "supreme head" of the church, a phrase obnoxious to the Catholics, she was now recognized as "supreme governor." No mere mincing over words, the distinction separated administrative from ministerial authority and was far more acceptable. The tests of heresy were now the Scriptures, the first four General Councils, and the decisions of Parliament.

The Act of Uniformity restored the second prayer book of Edward VI with small but important changes. The prayer against the pope, for instance, was omitted altogether. During the distribution of the sacraments, the more Catholic-sounding emphasis from the first prayer book was combined with the distinctly Protestant words from the second.*

When it came to instituting a new archbishop of Canterbury, the greatest care was taken to insure

---

*The words of administration from the first prayer book had been, "The Body of our Lord Jesus Christ which was given for thee, preserve thy body and soul unto everlasting life" . . . "The Blood of our Lord Jesus Christ which was shed for thee, preserve thy body and soul unto everlasting life." When the second prayer book was written, these were changed to "Take and eat this, in remembrance that Christ died for thee, and feed on him in thy heart by faith, with thanksgiving" . . . "Drink this in remembrance that Christ's Blood was shed for thee, and be thankful."

We should remember that both sets of words were penned by Cranmer, and that at his trial he maintained he had intended no difference in their meaning. But the fact is they have nearly always been interpreted as two quite distinct views of the Lord's Supper.

continuity with the past. Of the four bishops who consecrated Matthew Parker as successor to Cranmer, two had received their consecration during the reign of Henry VIII. Though Rome has argued against it, the intention was clearly to maintain an unbroken episcopal succession of leadership within the English church.

In 1563 the Forty-two Articles that Cranmer had drafted a decade earlier were revised and adopted as the famous Thirty-nine Articles, the statement of faith of the Church of England. These Articles of Religion are a magnificent summary of Reformation theology. (If *The Book of Common Prayer* is read in light of them, it is indisputably Protestant. Without them, it is deliberately ambiguous at several critical points. It is as if Elizabeth made certain that the sharp lines drawn in the area of doctrine were blurred in the area of worship to accommodate as many people as possible. Certainly, it has been the neglect of the Articles that has permitted such a diversity in the interpretation of the same liturgy.)

In short, what evolved in the Elizabethan settlement was an inclusiveness that sought a middle way between Catholicism and radical Puritanism. The Church of England became the bridge church and had to be defended from attacks on both sides.

John Jewel, bishop of Salisbury, became part of the more radical wing of the Reformation when he realized that the primary attacks came from Rome. In 1562 he published his instantly famous *Apology for the Church of England.* His concern was to answer the question "Who are the innovators?" The answer? Not the Church of England, but the recent popes. Jewel contended that neither in the Scriptures nor in the undivided church of the first six centuries was there any doctrine of the supremacy of the pope. Yet by 600 the shape of Christian doctrine had become fixed in all other respects. It was the addition and not the rejection of papal supremacy that constituted heresy, contended Jewel. This being the case, the national churches should reject the leadership of the popes.

Some thirty years later Richard Hooker defended Anglicanism from a different threat—the excesses of Puritanism. Nothing is to be rejected, he maintained, merely because it was misused under Roman Catholicism. Whereas some of the extremists would have done away with all music, candles, vestments, gestures, set prayers, stained-glass windows, crosses, processions, absolutions, and benedictions, Hooker argued that none of these are wrong in themselves, though they had been wrongly used from time to time. For him the question was whether they might be used to edify, even apart from an express commandment of Scripture. How are we to judge? *By using common sense.*[12]

Hooker shared the Puritans' confidence in the Word of God as found in the Scriptures. This was clearly the basis of all doctrine. But where some refused to do anything that was not specifically mandated by the Bible, Hooker found room for "that characteristically Anglican thing"—the exercise of *reason*.

With Jewel arguing against the excesses of Rome and Hooker arguing against the excesses of Puritanism, the Anglican church adopted what might be called Reformed Catholicism. Bishop Neill summarizes what had been accomplished by the English church:

It had *maintained* the Catholic faith, as that is set forth in the Scriptures, the Creeds, and the decisions of the first four General Councils. It had *restored* the Catholic doctrine of the supremacy of Holy Scripture in all matters of doctrine and conduct. It had *restored* Catholic practice in the provision of worship in a language understanded of the people. It had *restored* Catholic practice in the encouragement of Bible-reading by the laity. In the Holy Communion, it had *restored* Catholic order by giving the Communion to the laity in both kinds, both the Bread and the Wine, instead of only in one kind, as was the practice in the medieval Church. In Confirmation and Ordination, it had *restored* Catholic order by making the laying on of hands by the Bishop the essential in the rite. It *aimed at restoring* the Catholic practice of regular Communion by all the faithful. It had *retained* the three-fold Order of the ministry: bishops, priests, and deacons. It had most carefully *retained* the succession of the bishops from the days of the Apostles. It had *retained* the liturgical order of the Christian year, though in a considerably modified and simplified form. It had *repudiated* the supremacy of the Pope, as that had developed since the days of Gregory VII. It *denied* that the Pope had authority to interfere in the civil affairs of States and to depose princes. It *claimed* liberty for national Churches, within the fellowship of Christ's Holy Catholic Church, "to decree Rites or Ceremonies" (Article XX). It *rejected* the scholastic philosophy, and the late medieval definitions, especially of transubstantiation, which had been based on it. It *rejected* late medieval ideas of purgatory, indulgences, and the merits of the saints. It *retained,* unfortunately, the medieval ideas of property, of jurisdiction, and of ecclesiastical administration. It *maintained* continuity of administration, most of the episcopal registers showing that the work of the Church was carried on through all the troubles without the intermission of a single day. It *claimed* to be a living part of the world-wide Church of Christ.[13]

* * *

In the fifteenth chapter of the Book of Acts, we read the story of the Council of Jerusalem, the first legal council in the history of the Christian Church. The issue being debated was the basis on which Gentiles could become Christians. There were those including the apostle Peter, who said that grace alone was adequate. Others contended that the rules of Old Testament Judaism needed to be enforced upon the new converts. Finally a middle way was found: rigorous adherence to a few essentials and freedom

41

of conscience in nonessentials. This same spirit of moderation has breathed through Anglicanism since the sixteenth century.

Questions for Thought and Discussion

1. What is the relationship between *The Book of Common Prayer* and the Thirty-nine Articles of Religion?

2. What does it mean to call the Anglican church the bridge church?

3. Do you feel comfortable with the Episcopal church's position of moderation—rigorous adherence to a few essentials and freedom of conscience in nonessentials?

4. What are the words of administration of the Holy Communion in the new revised version of the prayer book? How do they compare with the words of administration in the first and second prayer books? What theological interpretation is given to the words used in the first and second books?

5. In light of the differences between the Roman Catholic and Episcopal beliefs, do you think the two churches can reunite?

6. With so much controversy about ritual and its accompaniments such as candles and vestments, what do you see as the will of God for his Church? How important is ritual to you?

4

The Thirty-nine Articles

IT IS FREQUENTLY said that the Anglican and Episcopal churches are not *confessional*. That is, in contrast to certain other churches that have retained a statement of beliefs such as the Westminster Confession, they have no doctrinal standards. It is alleged that Anglican clergy may believe and teach almost anything (or almost nothing!). Sometimes this is said in criticism; sometimes it is said by Anglicans themselves as a matter of pride. Either way, it can be said only by ignoring or demeaning the Thirty-nine Articles of Religion found at the back of the prayer book.

It has become fashionable to do just this. A recent introductory volume on the Episcopal Church in the United States makes this extraordinary statement: "Since there is no dogma . . . diversity is possible. . . . Although the Thirty-nine Articles are deemed important enough to be printed as part of the Book of

Common Prayer, their subscription has not been required. They serve as possible guidance, but *they have no authority*."[14]

The truth of the matter is quite different. Before ever being ordained as deacon, prior to being ordained priest, and before being consecrated bishop, a man must pledge his conformity to the "doctrine, discipline, and worship" of the Episcopal church, which in effect means conformity to *The Book of Common Prayer*. And the constitution of the Episcopal church specifically includes the Articles of Religion as part of that book.

However, it is true that no specific endorsement of the Articles is required of candidates for ordination in the Episcopal Church, U.S.A. Many feel as Dr. Massey Shepherd that "it was thought the general oath taken before ordination . . . was sufficiently inclusive."[15] Elsewhere in the Anglican communion, however, a clergyman is required to subscribe to the Articles. Although the American version of the prayer book has been revised during the last few years, the Articles remain part of the official doctrinal standard for the Episcopal Church in the United States.

Virtually every confession of faith and every creedal statement has emerged from some particular theological controversy. In the early centuries when the Nicene Creed was being hammered out, the major issue concerned the doctrine of Christ. Accordingly, the major portion of that creed declares the orthodox teaching concerning his person: "God of God, Light of Light, Very God of very God; Begotten, not made; Being of one substance with the Father."

By the sixteenth century Christ's person was no longer a matter of dispute. Instead, the chief need, as Dr. Philip Hughes said, "was for a clear statement of the catholic faith concerning the work of Christ, the manner of the sinner's justification before God, the relationship between faith and works, the nature of the Church's ministry and sacraments, and the supreme authority of Holy Scripture in all matters of faith and worship."[16] Against the errors of the medieval Roman church on one side and the excesses of radical Puritans—the Anabaptists—on the other, the Thirty-nine Articles summarize the historic Anglican position. Shepherd says, "They are Protestant to the extent that they do not claim any doctrines as necessary to salvation except those that can be proved and established by the Holy Scriptures; but they are also Catholic in the sense that they do not reject the developed traditions of the undivided Church of the early centuries that are in accord with the mind of Scripture."[17] Of course, as Jewel demonstrated, the Anglican Reformers insisted that *they* were the true Catholics, for to be truly scriptural is to be truly Catholic!

The Articles may be grouped as follows:

1-5   treat the doctrines of the Trinity and the

Incarnation; they largely restate what was said in the historic creeds.

6-8   outline the basis of doctrinal authority in Anglicanism, namely the Scriptures and the Apostles' and Nicene Creeds. (The Episcopal Church, U.S.A., omitted mention of the Athanasian Creed in its version of Article 8).

9-18   deal with the nature of man and his salvation. We see here a clear reflection of both Lutheran and Reformed influence, particularly in Article 11, which affirms justification by faith alone *(sola fide),* and in Article 17, which declares our election in Christ by the sovereignty of God.

19-36   concern the doctrines of the church and the sacraments. Roman dogma is almost thoroughly repudiated in this section, though it must be admitted that under Elizabeth's conciliatory leadership several of Cranmer's more extremely Protestant statements were considerably softened. (The American church omitted Article 21 entirely, believing it to apply exclusively to the English situation.)

37-39   address the Christian's relation to the state. (The American church substituted a brief and general statement regarding the duty to obey legitimate authority for the originally lengthy Article 37 concerning royal supremacy.) Articles 38 and 39 in particular are directed against the Anabaptist teaching that all goods must be held in common and that a Christian may not take an oath in a court of law.

Beyond this simple outline, there are three major themes running through the Articles.

The first is the *authority of the Bible*. Article 6 says that "Holy Scripture containeth all things necessary to salvation: so that whatsoever is not read therein, nor may be proved thereby, is not to be required of any man, that it should be believed as an article of the Faith, or be thought requisite to salvation." It goes on to specify the books of the Old and New Testaments (and Article 7 stresses the continuity between them) and to commend the books of the Apocrypha as being valuable but not carrying doctrinal authority. As already discussed in chapter 1, it is Anglicanism's view of *authority*, more than any other single issue, that distinguishes it from Roman Catholicism, and from this all other issues flow.

Whereas the Roman church sees tradition (the decisions of councils and popes) as being equal to the Old and New Testaments, Anglicanism says plainly that the Roman church has erred (Article 19) and that the traditions of men are to be judged by the Word of God in the Bible. This is not to say that the church has no authority whatsoever, but rather that it has a derivative authority and must neither exceed nor contradict God's written Word nor set one portion of Scripture against another (Article 20). Traditions, rites, and ceremonies are legitimate as long as they do not violate God's Word. Anglicanism leaves to itself and any other ''particular or national'' churches the right to determine such things according to local needs (Article 34).

Several Roman doctrines are specifically repudiated: purgatory, pardons, the veneration of images and relics, prayers to the saints, transubstantiation, and the doctrine of supererogation* (Articles 14, 22, and 25), always on the basis that such doctrines are contrary to the teaching of Scripture.

The Anglican church embraces the Scriptures. It reads the Scriptures. It prays the Scriptures. It sings the Scriptures. And though some Anglican clergymen may have drastically departed from biblical teaching, they do not represent the mind of their church in doing so. Indeed, they are in direct opposition to it. One of the best-loved prayers of the Anglican church petitions:

> Blessed Lord, who hast caused all holy Scriptures to be written for our learning; Grant that we may in such wise hear them, read, mark, learn, and inwardly digest them, that by patience and comfort of thy holy Word,

---

*The doctrine that it is possible to accumulate merit by doing good above and beyond what God specifically requires.

we may embrace, and ever hold fast, the blessed hope of everlasting life, which thou hast given us in our Saviour Jesus Christ.

A second theme is *justification by faith*. The trumpet call of the Reformation is sounded in Article 11: "We are accounted righteous before God, only for the merit of our Lord and Saviour Jesus Christ by Faith, and not for our own works or deservings. Wherefore, that we are justified by Faith only, is a most wholesome Doctrine, and very full of comfort." Here again is a contrast to Roman teaching, with a strong repudiation of the merit of good works—indeed, an outright denial that they can even be called good works apart from faith (Articles 12 and 13). The Anglican Reformers recognized the phenomenon of doing the right thing for the wrong reason and argued that the surface appearance of benevolence or charity or righteousness may be a mask for self-serving motivations. They even said that works that "spring not of faith in Jesus Christ . . . have the nature of sin" (Article 13). Against the idea that we could pile up surplus merits by doing things above and beyond the call of duty (works of supererogation), Article 14 quotes Jesus, "when ye have done all that are commanded to you, say 'we are unprofitable servants.' "

Of course, "by faith alone" has often been misunderstood. Neither Luther, Calvin, nor any of the Anglican Reformers meant faith apart from the *ob-*

ject of faith. It is not one's fervency of faith that saves; it is Jesus Christ. But it is *by* faith that we lay hold of Christ's salvation; by faith we receive the gift Christ offers. "By faith alone" simply means by faith apart from works. There is nothing whatsoever we can do to earn it. Here the Anglican church repeats what Scripture itself proclaims so boldly, "For by grace you have been saved through faith; and this is not your own doing, it is the gift of God—not because of works, lest any man should boast" (Eph. 2:8, 9).

Thirdly, the Articles speak at length about *the nature of the sacraments*. The Anglican church recognizes only two sacraments, baptism and the Lord's Supper. Both of these are seen as having been specifically ordained by God as symbolic of the gospel and as means by which faith is strengthened. The Roman Catholic church recognizes five other sacraments—confirmation, penance, orders, matrimony, and extreme unction; but Anglicanism, while retaining these as sacramental rites, denies that they have the same status as baptism and the Lord's Supper—the sacraments of the gospel.

The Lord's Supper is a sacrament, not a sacrifice (Articles 28 and 31). "Transubstantiation (or the change of the substance of Bread and Wine) in the Supper of the Lord, cannot be proved by Holy Writ; but is repugnant to the plain words of Scripture, overthroweth the nature of a Sacrament, and hath given occasion to many superstitions" (Article 28).

"The Offering of Christ once made is that perfect redemption, propitiation, and satisfaction, for all the sins of the whole world, both original and actual; and there is none other satisfaction for sin, but that alone. Wherefore the sacrifices of Masses, in the which it was commonly said, that the Priest did offer Christ for the quick and the dead, to have remission of pain or guilt, were blasphemous fables, and dangerous deceits" (Article 31).

Eating physical bread and drinking physical wine is, in the sacrament of Holy Communion, a metaphor of putting faith in Christ. He is the source of all spiritual nourishment for the Christian, and thus, to partake of him is to "eat his body" and "drink his blood." The subtlety of this is easily missed, and there is no doubt that many Anglicans would perceive their Communion service to be expressing the same theology as the Roman Catholic Mass (that the bread is changed into Christ's literal body, the wine into his literal blood, and both are literally eaten and drunk in the celebration of the Supper). But this is refuted by the Anglican church: "The Body of Christ is given, taken, and eaten, in the Supper, only after an heavenly and spiritual manner. And the mean whereby the Body of Christ is received and eaten in the Supper, is Faith" (Article 28).

Christ's body and blood were offered once—on the cross. That sacrifice is not *repeated* at the Communion service; it is *celebrated*. The bread and wine are not *literally* his body and blood; they *represent* them as "certain sure witnesses and effectual signs of grace" (Article 25).

These are some of the distinctives of the Anglican church as expressed in the Thirty-nine Articles. To summarize: the Scripture is authoritative in all matters of faith and doctrine. It teaches that sinful man is justified by faith in the grace of God expressed in the sacrificial death of Christ. That death is commemorated and celebrated in the service of Holy Communion, in which the eating and drinking of physical bread and wine is likened unto the spiritual partaking of his body and blood.

We have admitted that the Articles of Religion have fallen into widespread disfavor and neglect. The clarity of their teaching has been obscured. The sharp, clear gospel they were intended to protect has sometimes been blunted and confused. Anglicans would do well to study again the Articles at the back of their prayer book.

*   *   *

In II Kings 22, the story is told of the boy-sovereign Josiah, who assumed the throne of Judah at age eight. In the eighteenth year of his reign, a certain book was found in the rubble of the Temple. It had been forgotten and ignored for generations, while all manner of idolatry and immorality had crept into Jewish worship. "And when the king heard the words of the book of the law, he rent his clothes" (v. 11). The king gathered all the people, from priest to peasant, and he read them the statutes of the Lord. Then Josiah vowed, on behalf of his people, "to perform the words of this covenant that were written in this book; and all the people joined in the covenant" (II Kings 23:3). The Scripture records one of the golden moments in the history of ancient Judah: the cleansing of the nation and the reestablishment of proper worship. It says of Josiah himself, "Before him there was no king like him, who turned to the Lord with all his heart and with all his soul and with all his might, according to all the law of Moses; nor did any like him arise after him" (II Kings 23:25).

Well might we in the Anglican communion rediscover our long neglected book and such leadership in our generation.

Questions for Thought and Discussion

1. What is a confessional church? Should the Anglican and Episcopal churches be considered confessional? Why?

2. What is "justification by faith alone"? How is it often misunderstood?

3. What is the difference between seeing the Holy Communion as a sacrifice and seeing it as a sacrament? What does this say about the true nature of a sacrament? How do you view the Communion service?

4. Should the Bible be the ultimate authority for all doctrine and ritual in the church?

5. Justification by faith or works is an historic argument. Did you realize that the Episcopal church took a definite position in this controversy? Do you agree with this position?

6. Should the Thirty-nine Articles be reemphasized by the Episcopal church? Should they be taught to confirmation candidates?

5

The Worldwide Anglican Communion

NOT VERY LONG AGO it could be said that the sun never sets on the British Empire. England reached out to embrace the world; and as its influence grew, so did that of the Church of England. But the Church of England was and is a national church. As the name implies, it was established and is partially controlled by the state. This political identity has both helped and hindered its evolution into a worldwide fellowship of independent churches.

At first there was no need to have separate churches in the British colonies; missionaries and chaplains were responsible to their various bishops back home. In fact, it has only been about two hundred years since there were any Anglican bishops outside the British Isles. But, just as the colonies attained independence, so did the many missions of the Church of England. Today there are nineteen national branches in what is called the worldwide Anglican communion—among them the Episcopal Church in the United States, the Anglican Church in Canada, and churches in Australia, Ireland, Scotland, South Africa, Tasmania, New Zealand, Wales, and the West Indies. Each has its own story to tell and each is self-governing and autonomous under God.

But they are Anglican churches, nonetheless. They own a common heritage doctrinally, liturgically, and, with local modifications, organizationally. More importantly, they are in communion with each other. In its simplest form, to be in communion with another church is to be able to receive the sacraments, particularly Holy Communion, in that church. This entails recognizing the validity of that church's orders of ministry. Technically, Anglicans are Christians in communion with their bishops, who are in communion with the archbishop of Canterbury. His spiritual authority is recognized throughout the Anglican communion, though he is not organizationally responsible outside the Church of England.

Anglicans base their worship on *The Book of Common Prayer*. The title suggests that the prayers are corporate and that the worship is common to all churches of this tradition. Of course, there are local differences. But, in spite of that, it is still *The Book of Common Prayer,* and a visitor from one Anglican church should immediately feel at home in another.

56

As a fellowship of churches, there is international identity, and the episcopal structure makes it possible for many churches to do together what none of them could do separately. On the level of a local diocese, many churches working together with their bishop provide for the funding of mission churches too poor to support themselves. A diocese can provide schools, hospitals, homes for the aged, social welfare, and rehabilitation centers well beyond the ability of a single congregation. On the national and international levels, episcopal cooperation has been most clearly manifested in the great missionary movement of the last century. Anglican missions were at the center of the astonishing African revival, where in Tanzania alone a new congregation was formed every week for more than twenty years! There have been major missionary efforts, often against tremendous odds, in China, Japan, Madagascar, Southeast Asia, and throughout the Moslem world. Through the Society for the Promotion of Christian Knowledge (SPCK), the Society for the Propagation of the Gospel (SPG), the Church Missionary Society (CMS), the South American Missionary Society (SAMS), and numerous other efforts, the Anglican communion is a growing, changing fellowship. It embraces nearly 70 million men, women, and children of every color, language, economic and social status, and geographical background throughout the world.

Being uniquely Catholic as well as Protestant, the

Anglican churches have also been leaders in the ecumenical movement. Beyond their fellowship with each other, they are in communion with a wider episcopal fellowship of churches, which have retained the office of bishop and the diocesan pattern of organization but have not emerged from the English experience.*

The continuing emphasis on the office of the bishop is the greatest stumbling block for the many Protestant denominations that have discussed formal union with Anglicans. There are within the Anglican church itself two very different views of its importance.

On the one hand, there has been a reintroduction of the extreme sacramentalist view that the unbroken line of ordinations back to the apostles is the only guarantee that a clergyman has been supernaturally empowered to perform priestly duties. There are those who would consider that unless a man has been ordained by a bishop of apostolic succession, his ministry—especially his sacramental ministry—is invalid.

But there is nothing in the Scriptures that will support so extreme a view. They, in fact, make no distinction between bishops and other elders—a

---

*Including the Church of Finland, the Church of South India, the Church of Sweden, the Lusitanian Catholic Church of Portugal, the Mar Thoma Syrian Church of Malabar (India), the Old Catholic Church of Europe, the Philippine Independent Church, the Spanish Reformed Church, the United Church of North India, and the United Church of Pakistan.

58

point we will explore more fully in chapter nine. The fact that a man has become a bishop differentiates him from other clergy administratively, not spiritually. The case for having an episcopal structure is more historical than it is theological.

As we have already seen, many things are possible when churches work together in a diocese that are not possible singly. But, how did the diocesan pattern first develop? Perhaps we can simplify it as follows. Suppose that a given local church begins a dramatic expansion. Soon people are traveling great distances for worship and finding that the building is too small to accommodate them when they arrive. A new building can be built, but the process cannot go on indefinitely. Even if it could, there would come a point when people are simply too numerous to know each other. Sooner or later another congregation must be formed in a neighboring community with its own pastor. Perhaps the original church will begin such a project as a missionary endeavor, with the new pastor responsible to the senior minister in the mother church. In just such an arrangement, we find the rudiments of an episcopal diocese.

We know that in the apostolic age there was only one congregation in a given geographical location (the church in Ephesus, the church in Colossae, the church in Corinth, etc.). As these local churches grew, smaller congregations were needed within the larger areas. But these were never viewed as isolated entities. They were integrally related to the mother churches from which they sprang. Their ministers were responsible to the senior ministers, the bishops, in those mother churches.

From a very early date in the subapostolic age, the bishop was viewed as the chief elder, the senior pastor or shepherd particularly charged with carrying on the apostles' tradition and mission. He was to preach not his own ideas, but what the Scriptures taught. He was to be the chief evangelist in his diocese. He was to preside at confirmations and ordinations. In short, though he delegated much of his responsibility to other elders, it was his responsibility to keep the church alive to its apostolic mission to go into the world and make disciples.

Calvin and some of the other Reformers on the Continent would have gladly kept the episcopal structure had they been able to control it, but this was not possible. When certain of the more radical Reformers opposed the episcopacy on theological grounds, the Church of England replied that they had gone too far.

The Anglican communion does not believe that Christian history is one huge accident in this regard. It believes that God himself was at work shaping the episcopal structure, and that it remains the best way of ordering the life of his Church. All this is reflected in a very important statement known as the Lambeth Quadrilateral.

In about 1870 an American, William Reed Huntington, published *The Church Idea, an Essay To-*

wards Unity, in which he argued that Romanism is an exaggeration, Puritanism a diminution, and liberalism a distortion of the church as God intended it to be. Anglicanism, he said, stands on four basic principles:

- the Holy Scriptures of the Old and New Testaments;
- the Apostles' and Nicene Creeds;
- the sacraments of baptism and the Lord's Supper; and
- the historic episcopate.

Together, he said, these principles make Anglicanism the best hope for reunion among the denominations.

In 1886 the General Convention of the Episcopal Church in the United States adopted these four principles as the basis for entering into "brotherly conference with all or any Christian bodies seeking the restoration of the organic unity of the Church." Two years later, the same basis was adopted at the international conference of Anglican bishops held roughly every ten years at Lambeth Palace, the London house of the archbishop of Canterbury. The Lambeth Conference is just that, a conference, and has no binding powers over churches in the Anglican communion. But, in its various forms, this Lambeth Quadrilateral has come to define the limits for ecumenical negotiations.

To envision the reunion of an episcopally structured church with churches of a nonepiscopal tradition, it is instructive to look at the Church of South India. The Church of South India was formed in 1947 as a merger of Anglicans, Methodists, Presbyterians, and Congregationalists. It preserved an episcopal structure by retaining the bishops of the Anglican tradition and including them in all ordinations subsequent to the merger. But it did not require reordination of ongoing clergy from the nonepiscopal traditions. Those who have become bishops in the Church of South India since the merger have represented all denominations that were party to the merger, and their consecrations have been at the hands of representatives of all denominations as well. Somewhat similar schemes in North India, Ceylon, Pakistan, and Nigeria have met with varying degrees of success and acceptance, although they have typically included a mutual commissioning, a reciprocal laying on of hands.

By 1920 the Lambeth Conference issued an "Appeal to All Christian People" for unity within the Body of Christ. It addressed itself specifically to the question of the Episcopacy. "It is not that we call in question for a moment the Spiritual reality of the ministry of those Communions which do not possess the Episcopate. On the contrary we thankfully acknowledge that these ministries have been manifestly blessed and owned by the Holy Spirit as an effective means of grace." The Appeal called for mutual recognition and commissioning but not for reordination.

Clearly it is a tragedy and an offense to the Lord who prayed that we all might be one to have a dozen or fifteen little congregations struggling independently in a given town, often next door or on opposite sides of the street. If they are to be reunited, some form of church governmental structure will be required. Anglicans believe the best form will be the ancient and traditional form of episcopal organization, with a bishop serving his diocese as senior pastor of the flock of Christ. Not all Anglicans would claim the episcopacy indispensible, but most would extoll its desirability in any ecumenical dialogue.

Anglicans and Episcopalians are engaged in ecumenical cooperation on many fronts. In addition to specific schemes for church reunion, they are active in the World Council of Churches and the National Council of Churches in America. For nearly twenty years, the Consultation on Church Union in the United States has attempted to bring together the churches of nine different traditions. So far, the attempt seems to have failed. But there are signs of progress—even in relation to the various churches of Eastern Orthodoxy, and in the Anglican dialogue with Rome. But, as we have seen, the problems are complex. It is extremely difficult to put history into reverse.

The intriguing thing is that on the local level great changes are taking place without waiting for the official sanction of a formal agreement. Where there used to be rigid strictures regarding who may and may not receive the elements in an Anglican Communion service, the rule increasingly seems to be: "If you confess Christ as Lord, and if you would be welcome at a Communion service in your own church, you are welcome here." Especially in America, closed Communion has given way to open Communion.

Standing as the bridge church between the Catholic and Protestant traditions, the Anglican Communion may yet fulfill Huntington's hopes and serve as the major catalyst for reunion. The Appeal of 1920 ended with the words, "We do not ask that any one Communion should consent to be absorbed in another. We do ask that all should unite . . . to secure and manifest to the world the unity of the Body of Christ for which he prayed."

* * *

This is the spirit of an incident in Luke in which the disciples asked Jesus to disavow the ministry of a man "because he does not follow with us" (Luke 9:49). Jesus' reply is a strong rebuke to the extreme traditionalist of Anglican, Roman, or Eastern Orthodox persuasion. "Do not forbid him; for he that is not against you is for you" (Luke 9:50).

Apostolic succession does involve the chain of ordinations back to the apostles, but the most important issue is truth. Are we following in the apostolic succession of truth? Are we faithful to the apostles' teaching?

It is rather like the parable of the ducks swimming

about in separate fenced-off areas of the same pond. When the owner floods it, the water rises above the fences, and all the ducks can swim together. Just so, when the Lord pours out his Spirit upon the church, Christians of very different traditions are able to rise above their denominational fences and come together with joy and freedom.

In one sense, it is blatantly tragic that there should even be an Anglican communion or a Roman Catholic church or an Eastern Orthodox or Presbyterian or Baptist or Congregational. In the imagery of the parable, it is very tempting to ignore the fences.

But this can also be dangerous. Some fences are there to protect the ducks. Without them, they might be swept over the dam. The quest for reunion must not compromise the truths of the gospel, truths for which the Anglican Reformers and many others lived and died. But if reunion is accomplished in the light of Scriptural truth, God's will that there be "one holy, catholic, and apostolic Church"—the Church of Jesus Christ—can truly be fulfilled.

Questions for Thought and Discussion

1. Why are some churches, entirely outside of England, still called Anglican? What do they have in common? How do they differ from non-Anglican churches?

2. What does it mean for churches to be in com-

munion with each other?

3. Why are bishops important to Anglicans? Should they be?

4. What are the advantages and disadvantages of a diocesan pattern of organization?

5. Discuss the formation of the Church of South India. How did that church deal with the problem of integrating episcopal and nonepiscopal ministries? What is the difference between mutual commissioning and reordination? Why is this issue important? Should it be?

6. What kind of authority does the archbishop of Canterbury have? Is he really a pope for Anglicans?

7. Is the Lambeth Quadrilateral a sound basis for ecumenical discussion with other churches? Could its fourth point be redefined in terms of the later appeal of the Lambeth Conference of 1920, which does not call for the reordination of clergy, just mutual commissioning? Should the Episcopal church make the continuance of the historic episcopate a prerequisite to union?

8. What are the pros and cons of the ultimate union of all Christian churches? How important are the theological and structural differences between them? Do you believe it is God's will that all Christian churches be reunited? Can this be done without losing the doctrinal truths of the Scriptures?

6

The Episcopal Church in America

THERE WERE OCCASIONAL Anglican services in the New World prior to the 1600s, but the official birthday of the Episcopal church in America is recognized as June 16, 1607. On that date Captain John Smith, of John Smith and Pocahontas fame, and some 104 other colonists celebrated the Lord's Supper with their chaplain to thank God for their safe arrival in Jamestown, Virginia.

For all its emphasis on the episcopacy, the American church had remarkably congregational beginnings. For nearly two centuries, Anglican worship was conducted without any bishops closer than England! Without a bishop, children cannot be confirmed, clergy cannot be ordained, and churches cannot be consecrated. Yet the need went unmet for 177 years. Generations of families came to the

Lord's Table without ever seeing a bishop, let alone being confirmed by one.

There were many Puritans and even some Anglicans who did not *want* English bishops, fearing that because of their connection to the king they might become agents of his imperialism. Conversely, the mother church was reluctant to consecrate any colonial clergyman whose allegiance to the king was questionable. So the muddle persisted, and as political troubles intensified, it worsened.

At the outset of the American Revolution, goodly numbers of clergy and laity chose to return to England or emigrate to Canada to maintain their relationship with both church and state. But no sooner had the fighting stopped than those who remained began laying the groundwork for an independent branch of what was becoming the Anglican communion.

In March, 1783, the Connecticut clergy chose the Reverend Samuel Seabury to be their bishop and sent him to England to seek consecration. They very wisely instructed him to continue on to Scotland and seek consecration there, if obstacles in England were insurmountable. Seabury did just this when the English Parliament would not set aside the requirement that every bishop take an oath of allegiance to the king. Thus it was that in Aberdeen, Scotland, on November 14, 1784, Seabury became the first Anglican bishop of the newly independent United States of America.

During his absence, an informal preliminary convention was held. It declared the American church independent of all foreign authority, political or ecclesiastical, but anxious to conform its liturgy to the Church of England. It affirmed the three traditional orders of clergy: bishops, priests, and deacons. And it determined that the laity should be involved with them in forming church laws. It proposed that all states should have bishops, and that all the bishops should sit in convention.

The first official convention followed shortly thereafter in Philadelphia in September, 1785. It was then that the church adopted the name: The Protestant Episcopal Church in the United States of America (PECUSA). After many attempts to change it, that remains one of the proper titles of the church, although in recent years it has become permissible to call it simply the Episcopal church.[18]

An immediate concern was to insure that there be just *one* Episcopal church in the United States, rather than one in each state or section of the country. Also, two more bishops needed to be consecrated, as three are ordinarily required to consecrate any other bishops. Fortunately, favorable relations were reestablished with the Church of England during the next year and a half. On February 4, 1787, the Reverend William White of Philadelphia and the Reverend Samuel Provoost of New York were consecrated bishops in Lambeth Chapel, London. Official recognition from the mother church helped to stabilize

her American offspring, and with its full comple-
ment of bishops, the Episcopal church was at last
equipped to handle its own affairs under God.

At first it was largely a church of the eastern
seaboard, lacking the flexibility to deal with a
rapidly expanding frontier. But slowly it grew and
matured and became ever more strongly a part of the
young nation's life. There were giants of the Episcopal church whose contributions will never be forgotten: Bishop Whipple, the apostle to the Indians of
Minnesota; Bishop Tuttle, forced to contend with the
Mormons in their self-styled land of Utah; Bishop
Griswold, whose evangelical efforts in the Eastern
diocese were so unstinting that it subdivided five
times before he died! And others: Bishops Hobart,
Moore, Kemper, and Polk, who were instrumental
in establishing Hobart College, Virginia Theological Seminary, Nashota House, and the University of
the South, respectively.

Much of the early impetus came from strong
evangelical leadership and biblical preaching.
Bishop R. C. Moore (1762-1841) was so strong a
preacher that one Sunday as he finished his sermon,
a member of the congregation interrupted him: "Dr.
Moore, the people are not disposed to go home;
please give us another sermon." He complied, but
they insisted on still more. Following his third sermon, Moore implored, "My beloved people, you
must now disperse—for, although I delight to proclaim the glad tidings of salvation, my strength is

exhausted, and I can say no more." In recounting the incident, E. C. Chorley comments that sixty communicants were added to the parish as a result of that service.[19]

There were many others. It was said that through the preaching of Bishop William Meade (1789-1862), the church in Virginia rose "as though from the dead."[20] And Bishop John Johns (1796-1876) is said to have kept Christ and his cross as the theme of his sermons, whatever his particular subject. "He saw all truth 'as it is in Jesus,' whether the fatherhood of God, or the sonship of man, or human brotherhood, or redemption, or duty, each truth presenting a different aspect as looked at in the mirror of Christ and his revelation."[21]

Typical of the evangelicals was Bishop Manton Eastburn (1801-1872). A commanding preacher, he used to say that "the Ritualists and the Broad Churchmen, like the cankerworm and the palmerworm, are destroying my diocese." He found ritualism abhorrent, and allowed no flowers in the chancel during his episcopal visitations. Having refused to visit a particular parish until certain changes were made, he finally came for confirmation. He addressed the confirmands as follows:

I have now, in compliance with the usages of our Communion, laid my hands upon you, and you have been confirmed. To what extent you comprehend the real nature of this act of dedication, and what instructions you have received respecting it, I do not know. I think it possible that you have been taught that this table is an altar, but it is not so, inasmuch as no sacrifice has ever been offered there, or ever can be. You may have been told by these gentlemen in the rear [the clergy] that they are priests in the Church of God. In any real sense you are as much priests as they are, for we are taught in the New Testament that all the faithful are alike priests in the kingdom of Christ. I made them what they are with a breath, and I can unmake them with a breath. They may have told you that it is your duty to confess your sins to them. You have as much right to insist that they should confess their sins to you. There is but one Being to whom we can go with our transgressions with any hope of being absolved.[22]

There were two grave setbacks to the evangelical cause in the life of the young church. The first grew out of the career of John Wesley and led to the Methodists breaking from the Episcopal and Anglican churches.

Wesley had gone to America as an Anglican missionary in the late 1730s, but he returned to England when his efforts were singularly unsuccessful. Some Moravian Christians invited him to a meeting in Aldersgate Chapel, London. As he listened to a reading of Luther's *Preface to the Epistle to the Romans*, he suddenly grasped the great Reformation principle that had eluded him: the just shall live by *faith*. Having been a clergyman for more than a decade, Wesley counted the Aldersgate experience as his conversion. He said his previous religion, for all its zeal, had been a matter of self-effort and good works. Now, he wrote in his journal, "I felt my heart strangely warmed. I felt I did trust in Christ, Christ alone, for salvation, and an assurance was given me that he had taken away my sins."

Wesley began proclaiming the gospel with a clarity and power he had never known. His brother Charles, who was also ordained, had been converted just three days previously. Together with a third Anglican clergyman, George Whitefield, who had recently returned from America, they began the practice of preaching in the open air all up and down the face of England.

They called men and women to personal commitment to Christ and developed the "method" of strengthening the converts through disciplined personal devotions and midweek fellowship meetings designed to supplement regular church worship. This method was not very new; Wesley had been using it since his undergraduate days. But these "Methodists," as they were called, were increasingly criticized for it and for their enthusiasm and emotionalism. The open-air preaching was particularly controversial, sometimes drawing crowds of over twenty thousand. And repercussions were quickly felt in America.

Whitefield returned frequently to the colonies and was a key figure in the Great Awakening that swept the New World. On both sides of the Atlantic, growing numbers of young men felt called as circuit-riding preachers on the American frontier.

Note that these Methodist circuit riders were Anglicans; their doctrine and piety was that of the English Reformation, adapted to a pioneer life-style. Wesley never intended to form a new denomination; he repeatedly looked to the English bishops to sanction the rapidly expanding missionary activity and to ordain the laymen he was sending to America. But to no avail. The controversy was too heated, the "emotionalism" too strong, and the expansion too dramatic. The bishops refused their approval.

After years of frustration, Wesley decided to ordain the circuit riders himself. Many of his closest associates begged him not to take this precipitate action, but he became adamant. Unable to go to America himself, he sent a Dr. Cook as superintendent to ordain the preachers. The break was irrevocable, although some Methodists insisted for several years afterwards that they were still loyal Anglicans. It was also tragic and perhaps altogether unnecessary. Had Wesley just waited two months longer, Samuel Seabury would have been consecrated, and he would have been willing to ordain the preachers who were properly qualified. How much stronger both churches would have been had that decision not been made! As it was, a tremendous amount of evangelical impetus was drained away from the already struggling Episcopal church.

A second setback came a century later with the Oxford Movement and the subsequent breaking away of the Reformed Episcopal church.

Between 1834 and 1841 a series of controversial tracts, calling for the reintroduction of Roman Catholic traditions, were published in England. The initial emphasis was on traditions that had developed before the Reformation, but later some writers began to promote post-Reformation elements as well. The Tractarians taught that episcopacy was essential to the very being of the church, and that it, like other traditions that developed during the course of Christian history, was contained in embryo in the Bible itself. If the church evolved from the apostles, so its teaching and practice was a development of theirs. The church was therefore infallible in its interpretation of Scripture, they reasoned, and the Bible could only be read accurately in the light of tradition. John Henry Newman, the Tractarians' most influential spokesman, even attempted to reconcile the Thirty-nine Articles with the official dogma of Roman Catholicism!

Newman and a number of other Oxford leaders eventually moved to the Roman Catholic fold, but many stayed and attempted to reestablish first the ceremonies and then the theology behind them.

Evangelicals could agree with the Tractarians on a number of issues, and Tractarians were particularly successful in the United States, where there was a widespread neglect of the sacraments. Perhaps

America's weak episcopal beginnings without a bishop's leadership fostered an irreverence and sloppiness in worship and liturgy. The Oxford Movement did much to recapture a sense of the majesty of God and the wonder of his involvement in his Church throughout the ages. This was especially needed on the American frontier where a radically individualistic understanding of the gospel needed to be balanced with an appreciation of the corporateness of his Body the Church. It has been said that the Oxford Movement did for the church what the Evangelicals did for the individual: make Christ a living reality.

However, within the Oxford Movement a growing number of Anglican and Episcopal leaders began to view the Reformation itself as a mistake, a travesty that had to be reversed. They set about to do just that. Nearly every bit of external ceremonial Episcopalians take for granted today was reintroduced in the last 125 years to recast the church in a more Catholic mold. For instance:

- Cassocks and surplices again replaced the academic preaching gowns that had become standard throughout America.
- Candles and flowers began to adorn Episcopal sanctuaries.
- Communion tables began to be made of stone and called altars (whereas English church law insisted they be made of wood and be movable to signify they were tables, not altars).

76

- Embroidered frontals were hung on the altars.
- Clergy began wearing colored eucharistic stoles and then full-fledged eucharistic vestments.
- Crosses and even crucifixes began appearing.
- Divided chancels replaced the old three-tiered central pulpits.
- It became common to read the Epistle and Gospel from opposite sides of the altar and to face the altar for some prayers.
- Vested choirs and acolytes appeared.
- The clergy began bowing, genuflecting, making the sign of the cross, performing ablutions (washing their hands and the communion utensils during the service itself), and elevating the bread and wine as an offering to God.
- In many places, incense was used.

The point is that none of these has an unbroken history in the Anglican or Episcopal church. They were all reintroduced during the 1840s and afterward.

The evangelicals generally viewed them with horror. Bishop C. P. McIlvaine warned the Ohio Convention in 1843, "the whole system is one of church instead of Christ; priest instead of Gospel; concealment of truth instead of 'manifestation of truth'; ignorant superstition instead of enlightened faith; bondage, where we are promised liberty—all tending directly to load us with whatever is odious in . . . priestcraft, in place of the free, affectionate, enlarging, elevating, and cheerful liberty of a child of God.''[23]

During the same year, Bishop Philander Chase wrote that approximations to Rome were not innocent. ''The disposition to reform the Reformation is as dangerous as it is foolish, and should receive a rebuke from every Protestant bishop.''[24]

But still the movement grew, with many leaders, including Bishop Seabury, becoming sympathetic.

Theology began to reflect the changes. It was only now that the doctrine of the real presence of Christ in the Communion elements was again articulated. The House of Bishops circulated a pastoral letter following the General Convention in 1868, condemning any doctrine that localized the bodily presence of Christ in the Communion elements.[25] The fact that the bishops issued such a statement shows the growth of this belief.

Today, the doctrine of the real presence is considered nearly dogma in many Episcopal circles.

The doctrine of baptism was changing as well. The ancient use of the word *regeneration* was to designate a change of status or position. *Baptismal regeneration* symbolized or expressed one's membership in the community of faith. Following the Great Awakening, however, *regeneration* came to mean personal conversion, an internal not an external happening. The evangelicals found themselves less and less happy with the baptismal office, particularly in using it for children. It seemed to them that the pronouncement "Seeing now . . . that this Child is regenerate" made the new birth mechanical, a matter of automatic grace. They began to omit phrases that they considered objectionable from the office.

The more Catholic, or Anglo-Catholic, view was that it was precisely the nature of a sacrament to be automatic. They turned the question into a battle by bringing a number of evangelicals to ecclesiastical trial for their omissions.

In the face of this building pressure, a number of key evangelicals defected. On December 2, 1873, Bishop George D. Cummins, eight other clergy, and nineteen laymen broke away and organized the Reformed Episcopal Church.

For most of the other evangelicals, this was worse than losing the Methodists. Most felt Cummins and the others had given up too soon and too easily. They recognized that though the break was a small one, and never became large, it took away key leadership. Over the years it also drained off an evangelical impetus that is needed in the Episcopal church. Inevitably, our church has moved even farther in the opposite direction.

The issue today is not the externals of ceremony. Evangelicals recognize that one can appreciate candles, flowers, and a considerable amount of ceremony; such things can lend dignity and beauty to a service. The real issue is the theology behind the ceremony, and here there are great differences.

The extreme sacramentalist, like the Roman Catholic, believes that the Bible cannot be properly interpreted except in the light of tradition. This is a clear renunciation of the Reformation principle of *sola Scriptura*. Evangelicals see this as the central issue, because once the authority of the Bible has been compromised, everything else is open to distortion, abuse, and compromise.

Particularly in regard to the sacraments, evangelicals believe that a critical distinction has been lost. According to the Bible and the Thirty-nine Articles, the sacraments are "effective signs" and "certain sure witnesses" of grace (Article 25). They do not confer grace automatically. But they are the outward and visible expression of the grace given by God to repentant believers for their forgiveness and renewal.

The extreme sacramentalist, however, says something quite different. He offers Eucharists—sometimes even "Masses"—with "special intention," which seems to imply the accumulating of merits in the process. He "reserves" the sacrament and, in some cases, even "adores" it, though this is thoroughly condemned in Article 28. His doctrine seems indistinguishable from that of transubstantiation.* His view of infant baptism makes rebirth

---

*The sophistical arguments about the difference between transubstantiation and consubstantiation do not alter the fact that both doctrines teach that the literal, physical body and blood of Christ are in the Communion elements. The biblical teaching is that Christ is "really present" surely, but spiritually, in the hearts of true believers.

automatic. He prays for the dead beyond the warrants of Scripture.

More generally, it is the abandonment of biblical authority that has led to all manner of foolishness in the ethical, moral, and political agenda of the church. The great issues of our day are addressed all too often on the basis of humanistic and rationalistic philosophy rather than the prophetic "Thus saith the Lord." An analysis of the books and articles, lectures and sermons of many Episcopal leaders in the twentieth century would support this contention. Whatever the issue—civil rights, international relations, the role of women, economics, abortion, apartheid in South Africa, fire-bombing in Vietnam, homosexuality, corruption in government, or what have you—biblical issues are all too often being addressed politically, rather than political issues biblically.

The looseness of our church was epitomized in the 1960s by the sad case of the late Bishop James Pike. Prior to leaving the church voluntarily, Pike had come to the point where he disavowed the divinity of Christ, the Virgin Birth, the miracles, the Resurrection, the Second Coming, eternal life, the last judgment, and heaven and hell. He said the Bible was "no more than a handful of stones." Yet he was neither censured by the House of Bishops nor stripped of his episcopal authority.

Having argued in chapter 5 that the Thirty-nine Articles are still binding, we now must admit that in practice everything from unreformed medieval dogma to outright unitarian humanism can be found within the Episcopal church. It is time for a new Reformation.

* * *

In speaking to the Sadducees one day, Jesus said, "Is this not why you are wrong, that you know neither the Scriptures nor the power of God? (Matt. 22:29). Is this not why churches go wrong, as well?

Questions for Thought and Discussion

1. How were the beginnings of the Episcopal church in America tied to the politics of the Revolution? How did the effects of this tie make the American church more open to the Oxford Movement?

2. What are the beliefs of the evangelicals? The Tractarians? Which of these beliefs seem true to you? What is the main controversy today between evangelicals and extreme sacramentalists?

3. Why did the Methodist and the Reformed Episcopal churches break away from the Episcopal church? How did their leaving affect the church?

4. What did the Oxford Movement contribute to the Episcopal church? What were the changes that resulted from the effect of this movement? Were these assets or detriments?

7

The Anglican Church in Canada

by Canon Harry Robinson
Little Trinity Church, Toronto

And we are determined by the help of God to hold and maintain the doctrine, Sacraments and discipline of Christ as the Lord hath commanded in His Holy Word, and as the Church of England hath received and set forth the same in the Book of Common Prayer . . . and to transmit the same unimpaired to our posterity.
—from the Solemn Declaration, 1893

Anglicanism in Canada was already 315 years old when this pledge was made by the church. Robert Wolfall, a chaplain to the expedition of Martin Frobisher, was the first to celebrate the Lord's Supper on Canadian soil. The year was 1578.

The remote spot on the barren Arctic coast where Wolfall and the explorers, searching for a shorter passage to the Far East, stopped to worship is now called Frobisher Bay. Here, a cathedral shaped like an igloo serves the largest Anglican diocese in the world—2,750,000 square miles. Most of the members are devout Eskimo *(Innuit)* who found Christ through the sacrificial efforts of Anglican missionaries. These missionaries traveled by foot and dogsled to the sparse settlements of these nomadic people, learning the language and dialects and translating the prayer book and Bible into Eskimo.

In these early years, Canada was called British North America, and the Anglican church, the Church of England in Canada. Its first responsibility was to establish the church from coast to coast in every district and community, a prodigious task, considering the vast distances.

Church missionaries traveled the inland waterways of the Great Lakes and the Hudson Bay, crossing the prairies by horse and half-ton truck from the Lake of the Woods to Rocky Mountain House. The prayer book, the Scriptures, and the ordered life of worship were carried by ship up the mountainous coasts of British Columbia and by train to the tiny villages and emerging cities along the great east-west railway lines. The missionaries sought to maintain the settlers' faith and to convert the Indian and Eskimo peoples.

As a result of their efforts, the General Synod of the Anglican church is today composed of fishermen from the north shore of the Saint Lawrence; sophisticated and cultured Anglicans from the big city churches of Toronto, Vancouver, and Montreal; rugged folk from mining and railway towns, farm communities, and Indian reserves; bishops from twenty-eight dioceses; and four archbishops from the ecclesiastical provinces of Canada, Rupert's Land, Ontario, and British Columbia.

Not only is there a great mosaic of peoples but also of religious beliefs and practices. There are those who hold to Catholic traditions imported from the American church and the Church of England, while others of the Protestant Irish tradition shun candles, crosses, stoles, and processions in favor of biblical preaching, political involvement, evangelical doctrines, and rugged individualism.

Today Anglicans are the third largest denomination in Canada, after the Roman Catholic Church and the United Church of Canada, a union of Methodists, Presbyterians, and Congregationalists. The Catholic church was established by early French settlers, and it became a home church to countless European immigrants, making it almost as large as all the other denominations together.

Canada has not blended its nationalities as the United States has. It has always had conflicting national identities, and for this reason, the origins of the various forms of Anglicanism can easily be traced.

The first form is the colonizing church, seen in provinces such as Quebec where Anglicanism is still a scattered denomination. French-speaking Roman

Catholic communities are more numerous and seem a more indigenous part of this area.

Here the Anglican church continues to draw its life from England, preserving high standards of English church music and patterns of ritual. For a long time, bishops were appointed by the archbishop of Canterbury, and English accents and training still mark many of the church's leaders.

This is not meant to undermine England's tremendous contribution to the Canadian church. But it does show one reason why Christianity has had difficulty taking root among the indigenous peoples. It has been so much easier to import vintage Anglicanism from England or dynamic Episcopalianism from the United States.

Other colonists came to Canada when the loyalists fled the American colonies during and after the Revolution of 1776. These people had given up their wealth, their homes, and their land to stay under the British crown and were intensely loyal to the Church of England.

From Nova Scotia to Detroit, there are lovely miniature English churches, built by loyalist settlers as a focus for their worship and a symbol of their determination to remain British. This environment so emphasized the British way of life and their traditions that evangelistic work and the opening of the church to others became secondary.

Among these loyalists were many Mohawk Indians under the leadership of Joseph Brant and their influential Anglican chaplain John Stuart. They left what is now New York State and emigrated to Canada, settling around Brantford, Ontario. There you can still see the famous Chapel of the Mohawks and their beautiful communion silver, a gift from Queen Anne.

In 1793 Bishop Jacob Mountain was sent from England to strengthen the position of the established church against the local dominance of Roman Catholics in Quebec. When he arrived, he was greeted by the Roman Catholic bishop, who kissed him on both cheeks and welcomed him to the cure of the Anglican flock. Ironically, this very cordiality established a pattern that inhibits the life and ministry of the Anglican church. Normal outreach is held back for fear of offending some other ecclesiastical body that might have first right to evangelize but has never done so. Thus, Christian churches in Canada have often maintained cultural and racial origins rather than proclaiming oneness in Christ.

The Irish famine of the 1840s brought more Anglicans to Canada and established a second form of Anglicanism. These Irish immigrants brought with them a strong brand of Protestant Anglicanism that led to the basic dichotomy behind Canada's political and religious life.

On one side was the French Roman Catholic community of Quebec; on the other, the English-speaking political Protestantism of Upper Canada, now Ontario. The political confusion in Northern

Ireland today is reflected in Canada by the practical extinction of the Protestant Orange Order, which was a part of most Ontario communities and a significant force within the Anglican church.

Canadian Irishmen established the low-church tradition in Canada, put stronger emphasis on preaching, and provided congregations to carry out evangelism and evangelical work.

So strong was the Irish influence that until the prayer book revision of 1918, the church was titled "The United Church of England and Ireland." Irish Anglicans still remind their English brothers that the See of Armagh is older than the See of Canterbury.

When the Oxford Movement became influential in England, it slowly introduced crosses and candles, altars and confessions, and other Romish rites into the Canadian church. Here these practices ran into the canons of the Church of Ireland where, after centuries of being the minority church in a predominantly Catholic country, they knew how to counter Romish inroads.

When Toronto was incorporated in 1837, the population was so predominantly Irish that it was almost called New Dublin. It is not surprising that Toronto is the one place in all Canada where the traditions of high and low church are most vigorously maintained. Parishes there are often more Catholic and sometimes more Protestant than anywhere in Canada.

The third form of Anglicanism is seen in the work

of missionaries among the widely scattered native peoples. The names of the twenty-eight dioceses ring with adventure, hardship, and devotion. There is Moosonee and Athabasca, Yukon and Kootenay, Niagara and Newfoundland, Keewatin and Rupert's Land, Cariboo and Qu'ppelle. Behind each of these names lies a story of missionary endeavor directed by societies such as the Society for the Propagation of the Gospel, the Church Missionary Society, and the Society for the Propagation of Christian Knowledge. These great English societies organized an endeavor that was peculiar to the needs of the Canadian church. Four of them are still serving Canadians today.

The Canadian Sunday School Caravan Mission, which has existed for fifty years, provides a roving Sunday school for young people. Trucks especially adapted as home and headquarters for teams of two visit the isolated settlements of the prairies bringing Sunday school instruction to the children. The mission also mails material to children who are completely isolated.

A seagoing chaplain visits the rugged mountainous West Coast from Victoria north to the Alaskan Panhandle under the auspices of the Columbia Coast Mission. When the boat arrives, it's always Sunday, and the instruction, services, and social and medical work begin.

Schooling in the colonies of British North America was the special interest of the Colonial and

Continental Missionary Society. This British society began schools in Newfoundland, which was a separate British colony until 1949. However, this colony was strongly tied to the Anglican Church of Canada, and its school system is still dominated by the church.

This British society, now called the Commonwealth and Continental Missionary Society, continues to have supporting interests in the life of the Canadian church. But it made its greatest contribution by sending young men from the British Isles to train in Canada (particularly at Emmanuel College, Saskatoon) for work in missionary areas here.

Contemporary discussions of native rights have questioned the benefits of some of the great Indian schools. These schools brought children together from all over the North and West of Canada to receive basic and secondary education. At the time, this was thought to be a necessary way of evangelizing the native peoples. However, any advantages must now be seen in light of its disruptive impact on family and tribal life.

The Church Army, a missionary thrust devoted to evangelism, has been training men and women for a rugged and mobile ministry in places where the parish structure does not fit. The army supervises work among the young and in prisons, evangelistic missions, and communities without a church. Many Church Army officers get their training in these difficult assignments, go on to ordination, and prove to be reliable pastors, benefiting the ordained ministry of the church.

Some great heroes of the Canadian faith were associated with these missionary societies. John Horden, missionary bishop to Moosonee, effectively preached among the Indians of James Bay. Henry Budd, a graduate of an early Indian school, was the first North American Indian to be ordained, in 1850. John West, the pioneer missionary to the Red River, Edmund James Peck, who took the gospel to the Arctic, and countless others are part of this unwritten story.

The best and the worst in the Anglican church today is seen in Toronto. Here the old aspirations to be the established church still exist. Here the national headquarters determines missionary, social, and financial policy. In doing so, it creates the theological ferment that sometimes goes bad, and sometimes produces good wine.

Much of the current tension is represented by the opposing viewpoints of two Anglican theological colleges, accidentally located side by side in Toronto. Wycliffe College was founded by a group of evangelical churchmen who vigorously opposed the kind of monarchical episcopacy and priestly domination that was characteristic in the late nineteenth century. However, this national theological college has had a difficult struggle maintaining a conservative biblical stance while located in the heart of Toronto University, where Roman Catholic, Presbyterian, and United churches all have their centers of almost purely academic theology.

Neighboring Trinity College, founded by John Strachan, became established as the center of strong churchmanship and rationalistic philosophy. A diocesan college with strong ceremonial tradition, it has been dominated in recent years by a deep interest in the church fathers and their writings and a strong emphasis on philosophy and liberalism.

Reaction to this theology at Trinity led to the founding of two more theological colleges—Huron College in London and Emmanuel in Saskatoon. Both were built by Irish churchmen to train men for the biblical ministry of evangelism as well as pastoral work.

The Anglican Church of Canada in the 1970s is torn by several issues. The women's liberation movement has opened the whole question of the meaning of ordination. Initiation rites, baptism, confirmation, and entrance to communion have forced us to face what it means to be a Christian and a churchman in a secular and pluralistic society.

The massive failure of effective church union has forced people to examine the very basis of our denominational existence. Liturgical unrest threatens our solidarity and opens for renewed study the prayer book, which was last revised and adopted by the Canadian church as recently as 1963.

It is difficult to answer these demanding questions from within a strong, hierarchical, institutional, and traditional structure. Rather than cope with these limitations, many people move out of the formal and historic denominations into more spontaneous structures, where these questions are largely ignored.

Moreover, the church in reacting to these issues is partially paralyzed by the difficulty of effecting change in such a widespread and diverse membership. Church headquarters on Jarvis Street in Toronto often seems to deal with questions and policies that are removed from local parishes and dioceses.

Their more recent policies have aroused considerable opposition in business and industry. It is not hard to find the unusual situation of laymen challenging pronouncements from church headquarters, not from within the local congregation but from the perspective of their secular occupations.

It has been characteristic of our church that policy comes from the top. In contrast to this, there is a new dynamic and charismatic sense of the church and its purpose at the grass roots level. While the official church is trying to influence national and international economic policies, church members are interested in a faith to meet their daily needs. Locally, there is a new openness to small-group Bible study and prayer, an interest in biblical preaching, a recognition of the spiritual gifts of the laity, and a swing away from strong central leadership to responsible membership in the congregation.

* * *

A famous statement from the General Synod of

1963 said that Anglicanism in Canada was simply "an accidental configuration of history which will disappear in ten years." Accidental though it may be, it continues to survive and serve God.

Canada's official motto, "From sea to sea," comes from the biblical quotation, "May he have dominion from sea to sea, and from the River to the ends of the earth!" (Ps. 72:8). The Anglican Church of Canada is a part of God's purpose in this land.

Questions for Thought and Discussion

1. How are the histories of the Episcopalian church of the United States and the Anglican Church of Canada alike? How do they differ?

2. How has the Episcopal church influenced the Anglican church in Canada? How has the Anglican Church of England influenced the church in Canada?

3. What problems do the Episcopal church and the Anglican church in Canada share? What problems are unique to each one?

4. From these histories of the Episcopal and Anglican churches, do you think members of the Anglican communion around the world are similar?

8

Bishops, Priests, and Deacons

It is evident unto all men, diligently reading Holy Scripture and ancient Authors, that from the Apostles' time there have been these Orders of Ministers in Christ's Church—Bishops, Priests, and Deacons.
—from the Preface to the Ordinal,
The Book of Common Prayer (1928)

It may be evident what the three orders are, but there are a couple of major problems in saying it just that way.

The first is that the word *priest* means something entirely different in its usual connotation today than in New Testament usage. To most people, the word *priest* means one who performs sacrifices. *Priest, sacrifice,* and *altar* go together, precisely as they did in the Old Testament. But in the New Testament that

95

sort of priesthood has been abolished by the coming of Christ (Heb. 10: 9).

Jesus came as the great High Priest who offered, in the words of the Communion service, "a full, perfect, and sufficient sacrifice, oblation, and satisfaction for the sins of the whole world." His sacrifice was so entirely adequate that it neither needs nor can be added to. Therefore, the Greek word *hiereus* ("sacrificing priest") is never applied in the New Testament to Christian ministers. Dr. Leon Morris comments that the word *hiereus* "is used of Jewish priests and of priests of pagan religions, for in those religions officials did offer sacrifice. But there is no official in the Christian Church who may be spoken of as a sacrificing priest. . . . The fact that Christ is our great High Priest . . . means that His is the only priesthood in the Christian Church. . . . The conception of a priestly line, the members of which are the only people by whom sacraments can be effectively administered, is alien to the Gospel."[26]

Why, then, do we speak of priests in the Episcopal church? The word derives from the Greek *presbuteros,* from which we get *presbyter,* meaning elder. In Middle English *presbyter* had become *preest,* which finally evolved to *priest.* It is a great irony of our language that *priest* has come to designate two entirely diferent forms of ministry, one pertaining to the Old Testament dispensation, the other to the New. A Christian priest is a *presbuteros*—an elder; he is never a *hiereus*—a sacrificer.

The other problem in discussing bishops, priests, and deacons is that the New Testament uses the first two titles interchangeably. Bishops were presbyters, and vice-versa. For instance, Paul reminded Titus that he had left him in Crete to "appoint elders [*presbuteros*] in every town as I directed you, if any man is blameless. . . . For a bishop, as God's steward, must be blameless" (Titus 1:5-7). In Acts 20:17 Paul summoned the *presbuteros* of Ephesus to confer with him, but when they arrived, he called them bishops (v. 28). Peter wrote, "I exhort the elders among you, as a fellow elder. . . . Tend the flock of God over which you have been made bishops" (I Pet. 5:1, 2). And so on. In discussing the three orders of ministry in the Episcopal church today, we need to bear in mind that in the New Testament bishops and priests were not yet distinct from each other.

Both *bishop* and *presbyter* have lengthy pre-Christian histories. *Bishop* derives from the Greek word *episcopus*, which in Vulgar Latin had become *(e)biscop(us)*. *Episcopus* means overseer—literally, one who examines very closely, inspects thoroughly, is deeply concerned about and involved with something or somebody. It also designated one who visits, in the sense of making an official inspection tour. A visitation was an *episcope*.

In the Greek version of the Old Testament, all these variations of overseeing were applied directly to God himself. God was the Overseer, the *Epis-*

97

copus, the Shepherd and Bishop of Israel. In the New Testament, the chief *Episcopus* was Jesus. Peter wrote you "were as sheep going astray; but are now returned unto the Shepherd and Bishop of your souls" (I Pet. 2:25, KJV). Therefore, a bishop of the Christian church is one who exercises a pastoral ministry of caring for those entrusted to him in the name of Christ. Like God himself, like Jesus, he knows his people and is intimately involved in the details of their lives, and he gives of himself to meet their needs.

The word *presbyter* also has a lengthy prehistory in the Old Testament, beginning from the time when Moses begged God to raise up elders to share leadership with him (Num. 11). The Jewish elders were responsible for all aspects of life, both ecclesiastical and civil. They were elected by the community, installed publicly by their fellow elders, and they held office for life. They were not, even in the Old Testament, sacrificing priests, which was a separate order altogether. The elders' function was to deal with the Law: they studied it, expounded it, and administered it within the community.

These were the two concepts that came together as the apostles established presbyter-bishops to care for local congregations in New Testament days. The qualifications for such leadership were lofty. A presbyter-bishop must be a man of the highest moral integrity. His home life must be exemplary. He must be a mature Christian who practices what he preaches. He must avoid excess. He must not be a recent convert, lest he succumb to pride in his spiritual authority. He must be well known and respected even in the secular community so his reputation might bring credit to the gospel (I Tim. 3:1-7).

Such a man might legitimately aspire to leadership in the church, but he must never forget that it is primarily a leadership of *service*. Jesus said, ''If I, then, your Lord and Teacher, have washed your feet, you also ought to wash one another's feet. For I have given you an example, that you also should do as I have done to you'' (John 13:14, 15). And again, ''Whoever would be first among you must be your slave'' (Matt. 20:27).

These presbyter-bishops were to rule the church (I Tim. 5:17). They were to care for it (I Tim. 3:5). Other Christians were to be subject to them (I Pet. 5:5). However, they were not to ''lord it over'' their charge; they were commanded to exercise humility (I Pet. 5:3, 6). They were to pray for their people and to anoint the sick with oil, asking God for their healing (James 5:14). They were to teach and preach God's Word (I Tim. 3:2; 5:17). In short, they were to care for all the needs of the local church, both spiritual and physical.

The physical needs of the people gave rise to the other order of ministry—the diaconate. The word *deacon* comes from *diaconos*, meaning servant. We read in Acts 6 that the communal meals of the early Christians were becoming so large that the apostles found the simple business of distributing food a distraction to their primary task of preaching and teaching. They decided to "pick out . . . seven men of good repute, full of the Spirit and of wisdom" (Acts 6: 3) to wait on tables. This temporary measure was taken to meet a particular need, and it was probably not envisioned that a permanent order would emerge from it. Once the crisis had passed, however, the wisdom of institutionalizing a servant order became clear; and the diaconate became a regular feature in Christian organization.

It is important to notice that this was an altogether new element in the structure of the early church. There was nothing like it in Judaism. The apostles were quite ready to carry the idea of eldership over from the Old Testament in creating presbyter-bishops. But they were equally ready to institute something new, as they perceived the Holy Spirit leading them to shape the structure of the church.

It was, in fact, a continuing process of development that led the church to the separate orders of ministry as we know them today. By the time of Irenaeus, who became bishop of Lyons in A.D. 177, the threefold structure of ministry was well established. In the century between the New Testament and Irenaeus, the office of bishop became distinct from and superior to that of presbyter. And the office of deacon came to include specific liturgical functions.

In the course of those one hundred years, bishops

had increasingly come to exercise authority over large metropolitan areas that encompassed several congregations or parishes. Even today, an archbishop is called a "metropolitan." The bishop had become the *senior presbyter*. But now that he could no longer be intimately involved with all his parishes simultaneously, he delegated much of his authority to the local presbyters who were responsible to him. The presbyterate, or priesthood, emerged with all the bishop's powers except confirmation and ordination. In the bishop's absence, the priest presides over the life of the local congregation, particularly its worship, becoming celebrant at the Lord's Table and pronouncing absolution and benediction in the name of God.

The deacon has come to function as an assistant to the priest. He reads the Gospel, administers the cup, and dismisses the people. He visits shut-ins and hospital patients and takes the sacrament to those who cannot get to church. When licensed by the bishop, he preaches.

In the Anglican tradition, the diaconate is a separate order of ministry. There are those who elect to remain perpetual deacons all their lives, often combining their responsibilities with a secular vocation. This has made leadership available to small congregations who cannot afford to pay a full-time priest. However, the diaconate is also a necessary first step for those who want to become priests. One must serve as a deacon for a minimum of six months before being "raised" to priesthood.*

In turn, any priest is eligible to become a bishop, if he is elected at a diocesan convention called for that purpose. In the Episcopal church, a majority of the bishops (and standing committees) of the other dioceses must consent to the election. As we have seen previously, at least three bishops are required to lay hands on a new bishop for his consecration. At that time, he is given a Bible and instructed by the presiding bishop:

> Give heed unto reading, exhortation, and doctrine. Think upon the things contained in this Book. Be diligent in them, that the increase coming thereby may be manifest unto all men; for by so doing thou shalt both save thyself and them that shalt hear thee. Be to the flock of Christ a shepherd, not a wolf; feed them, devour them not. Hold up the weak, heal the sick, bind up the broken, bring again the outcasts, seek the lost. Be so merciful, that you be not too remiss; so minister discipline, that you forget not mercy; that when the Chief Shepherd shall appear, you may receive the never-fading crown of glory; through Jesus Christ our Lord. Amen.

Although there are archbishops in most other parts of the Anglican communion, the American church has adopted a structure like that of the United States

---

*Actually, the canons say a whole year, but that is usually reduced at the discretion of the bishop.

government. There are two houses that meet together every three years for a General Convention. One is composed of priests and laymen elected to represent their dioceses. It is called the House of Deputies and can be likened to the House of Representatives. The other consists of all active and retired bishops and is roughly like the Senate. The presiding officer of the House of Bishops is called the presiding bishop. He is chief among equals and carries great moral authority when he speaks. He is elected for a twelve-year term or until he reaches sixty-five, whichever comes first.

This, then, is the ministry of the Anglican and Episcopal churches. Preeminently it is a ministry of shepherding: of taking spiritual and even physical care of Christian flocks. Its basis is the ministry of God himself, and especially of Jesus. It is a threefold ministry whose details emerged in the subapostolic age but looks continually to the New Testament for an understanding of its calling.

There are two footnotes to be added.

The first concerns the laity as a whole. The Reformers used to speak of the "priesthood of all believers." The phrase reminds us once more that there is no separate priestly caste set apart to perform mediatorial functions on behalf of other Christians. Whatever the bishops, priests, and deacons are called to do, it is not that.

The phrase also suggests that *all* Christians are called to minister to one another in the Body of

Christ. All are to pray for one another. All are to comfort and exhort one another. All are to support one another. All are to offer themselves first to Christ and then in the service of one another.

The idea comes partly from the passage in Ephesians that is read at a priest's ordination. It says that God gave various leaders to the church "to equip the saints for the work of ministry" (Eph. 4:12). It is the saints—*all* the Christians—who are to do the work of ministry. The role of the leaders is to equip them for it. The biblical understanding of the church is not that the ministers are to minister, and the congregation is to congregate. There is a priesthood of all believers in which some are called to specific leadership responsibilities but in which all share corporately.

The New Testament pictures the church as a body with independent parts that need each other (I Cor. 12; Eph. 4, etc.). God's concern is to so distribute the gifts of his Holy Spirit that all work together for the common good. Too long has the church been crippled by expecting the clergyman to do everything. God's perspective is that in any given local parish there should be some who are evangelists, some with profound teaching gifts, some who are capable administrators, some whom he can use to heal supernaturally, some who counsel with his wisdom and knowledge, some who speak in tongues, some who interpret, some who prophesy, some who give with unusual generosity, and some who do all

104

the thankless little jobs that no one notices unless they are not done! Moving from a one-man-show mentality to anything that approaches this takes great sensitivity, but it is clearly God's pattern. Some churches are beginning to (re)discover it!

The other footnote concerns the role of women. There is no doubt that women exercised various kinds of ministry and leadership in New Testament days. A lady named Phoebe is mentioned as a deaconess (Rom. 16:1). Various prophetesses are mentioned (Acts 21:9), and one of the signs of the New Covenant is "your daughters shall prophesy" (Acts 2:17). Paul speaks of various women who labored beside him in the gospel (Phil. 4:3). We know that several of the churches met in the homes of women (Col. 4:15). When Paul gives his instructions regarding deacons (1 Tim. 3:8-13), it may be that the women are deacons themselves. The more mature women were expected to lead the younger ones, both by example and instruction (Titus 2:3-5).

In spite of all this, the New Testament places limitations on women's leadership in the church. Paul wrote, "I permit no woman to teach or to have authority over men; she is to keep silent" (1 Tim. 2:12). And again, "As in all the churches of the saints, the women should keep silence. . . . For it is shameful for a woman to speak in church . . . what I am writing to you is a command of the Lord" (1 Cor. 14:33-37).

The question of women's leadership is one of the

most hotly contested issues in the church today. Not only the Anglican churches, but virtually all Christian denominations are wrestling with this complicated and emotionally explosive concern.

The Episcopal Church of the United States authorized the ordination of women at its 1976 General Convention (after defeating it twice previously), but the debate goes on throughout the Anglican communion.

The question is much larger than we can hope to resolve in this chapter. But one thing is clear; the biblical issue is not that of a sacramental priesthood but of authority. The question is not whether a woman can be a *hiereus,* but whether she can be a *presbuteros*. There is nothing in the Scriptures that explicitly limits the sacramental ministry to male leadership. But there are these (and other) passages that throw into question the wisdom of asking a woman to become the rector of a parish or the bishop of a diocese. It is very sad that in most of the discussions these two issues have been hopelessly confused. God's guidance is needed to sort them out.

* * *

Mark records the poignant story of James and John asking Jesus for the privilege of sharing his glory by sitting on his right hand and his left in the Kingdom. He says that when the other ten heard of it, they were ''indignant''—coveting (perhaps) those positions of honor for themselves. Jesus rebuked them all, ''Your calling is to *service*—even unto death—not (necessarily) to glory.'' He went on to contrast the way in which pagan rulers loved to "lord it over" people with the calling of Christians to serve and to give their lives for others (Mark 10:35-45).

Much today is heard about the rights of people to be ordained. The Scripture knows no such language. There are different functions within the body of Christ, just as there are different functions within the Godhead. The Son is not the Father; he has always been and will always be subordinate to him. But subordination is not inferiority. Neither is there inferiority in the differences of calling within the church. God calls some to be bishops, some to be priests, some to be deacons, and *all* to be ministers. Those who are called into the ordained ministry have great responsibility entrusted to them. It is right that others respect them. But their estimation of themselves should always be: "We are unworthy servants; we have only done what was our duty" (Luke 17:10).

Questions for Thought and Discussion

1. How did the three orders of ministers in the Anglican church evolve? What are the specific functions of these orders? How has the present connotation of the word *priest* confused the priest's function?

2. What is the underlying concept of ministry in the Anglican church?

3. What does the author propose as the function of the laity in the church? Do you agree?

4. What is ordination for? What special rights and privileges does it confer?

5. What do you think the role of women in the church should be? Does the Bible specifically designate this role? Do you think the General Convention departed from Scripture by approving the ordination of women?

9

Liturgy:

the Work of the People

WHEN A VISITOR from a nonliturgical background first attends an Anglican or Episcopal church, his immediate reaction is often complete bewilderment. "They read everything out of a book," he says, "which was bad enough! But, to make matters worse, they kept jumping around in it, and I couldn't find my place. Beside all that, I never knew when I was supposed to stand, kneel, or sit. Confused? I was totally lost! I felt I was watching a performance, and I couldn't figure out how to participate."

Sometimes that last comment is even more forceful: "The whole thing seemed just a show put on by the minister and choir that hardly involved the congregation at all."

The reaction is understandable, but the intention is just the opposite. The purpose of liturgy is to involve people, not to exclude them. The word *liturgy* suggests this. The Greek *leitourgia* is a combination of *laos,* meaning people, and *ergon,* meaning work. So *liturgy* is the work of the people.

The prayer book might be thought of as a set of tools to help the people do their work. But some instruction is necessary to use the tools properly.

From the earliest days of the apostles, there were informal Christian gatherings that involved worship—prayer, singing, and even the Lord's Supper. But there was also, almost from the start, more formal worship when the whole church in a given area gathered together, with a presbyter-bishop presiding. And, as far back as we have records, such a formal worship service followed a set pattern.[27]

The first half was open to the public, except, of course, when the Christians had to go underground because of persecution. This part of the service included the opening greetings to one another, the reading of Scripture lessons and psalms, the sermon, and usually singing.

But then came a moment when all outsiders were dismissed, even those preparing to join the church who had not yet been baptized and confirmed.

The second half of the service was only for members; it included prayers and usually Holy Communion. Note that it was not only the Communion celebration but also the prayers that were restricted to Christians. According to Dom Gregory Dix, ''The church had a corporate duty to preach the gospel to the world and to witness to its truth. But prayer was another matter . . . . The church is the Body of Christ and prays 'in the name' of Jesus . . . . The world had a right to hear the gospel; but those who have not yet 'put on Christ' . . . cannot join in offering . . . prayer.''[28]

The time of prayer that followed reveals the origin of the Anglican liturgy. One of the leaders, a presbyter or deacon, would announce a topic and bid the people to pray. There then followed a period of silence during which people offered their private prayers regarding that particular topic. Sometimes various members of the congregation would pray aloud, leading in prayer from wherever they were. These individual prayers, whether silent or audible, were free or extemporaneous. After a few minutes, the leader would summarize or ''collect'' the prayers and then suggest another topic. Over the years the closing summaries became increasingly standardized, and the people would sometimes join the leader in saying the collects out loud. Even when the only voice was the leader's, the prayers were still corporate.

This was symbolized by the congregation's posture. They knelt during the time of private prayer but stood for the closing collect. Standing was the long established Jewish posture for priestly prayer. The congregation thus indicated that the collect was not merely being offered on their behalf, but they were participating in it. Here was a profound expression of the priesthood of all believers.

111

By the mid-fourth century, another method of participation was becoming popular: the use of litany. A litany is a series of short intercessions offered by a leader with a set congregational response, such as "Lord, have mercy upon us" or "We beseech thee to hear us, good Lord." This was a quite different form from the bidding prayers and collects, but the purpose was identical—to involve people in the work of prayer.

During the Middle Ages, however, a number of developments took place that weakened the participation of the laity. Probably most significant was imperial sponsorship of Christianity, dating from Constantine's conversion in A.D. 312. Great multitudes of people were baptized, confirmed, and declared Christian, sometimes on threat of death, who had never been converted. Obviously, a warm personal relationship with God became less and less the norm, and heartfelt personal prayer became the exception rather than the rule. People were herded into churches with no real desire or ability to participate. How different from the earlier dismissal of nonbelievers!

At this same time, a radically different understanding of the Lord's Supper was being developed. The simple Communion meal was becoming an elaborate and complicated celebration. The congregation were forced to be spectators of the clergy's performances, and the services in the West were by now in Latin, which very few of the people—indeed, relatively few of the clergy—understood.

Finally, the architecture of church buildings and cathedrals made real participation increasingly difficult. The congregation was now stretched out in an elongated building with a very high ceiling. People were no longer in an intimate family gathering. Even if there had been opportunities to speak or pray aloud individually, their voices simply would not have been heard.

All this began to change again at the time of the Reformation. In England the Communion table was moved to the center of the congregation (the people stood about it in the round). And through all the revisions of *The Book of Common Prayer*, one of the highest priorities has been to include the people. In the new American prayer book for instance, there is once again frequent opportunity for silent and audible extemporaneous prayer by members of the congregation, patterned after the ancient model.

We should remember, however, that even in its older forms, the purpose of the prayer book was to set down those prayers to be used in common, it is *The Book of* Common *Prayer*. It was never intended to be used in place of or to the exclusion of private personal prayer.

There is no doubt that a great deal is lost and the liturgy abused when the minister rattles through one collect after another (what is he ''collecting''?) rather than giving the congregation a chance to join him. But when topics are announced, silence is observed, and the congregation is encouraged to really pray—perhaps offering the collect with the minister, the liturgy becomes a magnificent vehicle for worshiping God.

Several observations might be made. First, we really do not have a choice of whether or not to use liturgy. By definition, when a congregation worships, it is doing liturgy—the work of the people. The comment at the beginning about a visitor from a "nonliturgical" background was a misnomer. The choice is not between liturgy or no liturgy but between having a set liturgy or leaving things to the spur of the moment and the discretion of the minister.

Experience tends to show that even churches that glory in their freedom from set liturgy inevitably fall into patterns of repetition. The minister often uses nearly identical phrases week after week, though they may not be written down anywhere. It could hardly be otherwise. Certain things are absolutely mandatory. God is to be praised at every service. He should be thanked for his graciousness and for the blessings he has bestowed. The sick and sorrowing should be uplifted in prayer. The leaders in government should be prayed for. The worldwide Church of Jesus Christ, in all its variety, its missionary endeavor, and especially in its tragic division, should be undergirded by prayer.

How many different ways are there to pray for these things? Is it really to be expected that the minister of a so-called free church is going to come up with a new pastoral prayer each time? In fact it is very likely he may be just as repetitious as *The Book of Common Prayer,* though it is unlikely he will be able to match its beauty.

A set liturgy provides another important element for worship: balance. Rather than reflecting merely a particular minister's feelings and insights at a particular moment, it incorporates a full expression of all elements of life with God as known by countless generations of faithful Christians. It requires discipline to use a set liturgy. We are told to "lift up your hearts," and we are expected to do so, whether or not we feel like it at that moment. We are told to confess our sins even if we do not feel particularly guilty. Perhaps this is part of what Paul meant when he said we are to be "casting down imaginations . . . and bringing into captivity every thought to the obedience of Christ" (2 Cor. 10:5, KJV). We worship God, not merely because we feel like doing so, but because he is worthy of worship. In fact, the word *worship* comes originally from *worth-ship.* And we are to discipline our worship according to what is true of him.

Finally, a set liturgy can have a teaching aspect that an entirely extemporaneous service lacks. This was extremely valuable during the periods of relative illiteracy in the church's history and still helps young children learn to worship.

C. S. Lewis somewhere observed that when the

minister's prayers are entirely extemporaneous, the congregation is forced to hold two irreconcilable attitudes at the same time. On the one hand, they want to worship God; they want to focus attention on him. But in order to do this, they must agree with what the minister is praying. This involves analyzing the prayers as they are spoken. One continually finds himself focusing on the prayer itself and asking, "Is this orthodox? Do I agree with this?" The prayer can then become an obstacle to worship, rather than a vehicle for it. Someone has remarked that when extemporaneous prayer is good, it is very, very good, but when it is bad, it is horrid.

There can be an equally horrid tendency in the opposite direction. There are those whose attachment to a given liturgy becomes so rigid that they miss the spirit altogether. There has never been a perfect liturgy, and there never will be. To become prayer book fundamentalists is a grave mistake, involving the attitude Jesus consistently rebuked in the Pharisees. Our Lord is not concerned with the externals of worship but that our worship be "in spirit and in truth" (John 4:23).

There will inevitably be change in the liturgy, if for no other reason than to adjust changes in our language. The word *prevent,* for instance, meant in the sixteenth century exactly the opposite of what it means today! Our concern ought never to be with what someone has called the seven last words of the church ("We never did it that way before.") but rather with the question: Is this the best contemporary vehicle for worshiping God in the light of biblical truth?

The recently completed revision of the American prayer book has been extensive and controversial, but even with its dramatically expanded flexibility, it retains the distinctive character of the first prayer book, drafted in the sixteenth century.

The Book of Common Prayer was designed to contain services for virtually every occasion. It begins with the daily office, a series of worship services for morning, noonday, and evening prayers that are monastic in origin. Eight separate services were observed in the medieval monasteries each day: lauds, prime, terce, sext, none, vespers, compline, and matins. At the time of the Reformation, these eight were combined into two services of prayer and Scripture to begin and end the day. Alternative and additional services have been included in the new book. When it is used daily, nearly the entire Bible is read on a three-year cycle, and the Book of Psalms is rehearsed each month.

The new prayer book also includes a litany; collects and services for special days during the year; services for holy baptism, Holy Communion, and events and crises in the life of an individual or family (confirmation, matrimony, visitation of the sick, etc.); and services for ordaining clergy, consecrating churches, and instituting a clergyman as rector or vicar of a parish.

In both the daily office and the order for Holy Communion, there are now alternative services that use either traditional or contemporary language.

The Book of Psalms is reprinted in its entirety, followed by still more optional prayers and thanksgivings. A catechism or outline of the faith is included, especially for use in preparing for confirmation. Finally, there is a historical-documents section containing, among other things, the Lambeth Quadrilateral and the Thirty-nine Articles of Religion.

The basic rule regarding posture has traditionally been "We kneel to pray, sit to learn, and stand to praise." But there are exceptions to this, such as standing while the Gospel is read during Communion service. Once again, the critical thing is not the externals but a question of our attitude. We gather to "worship the Lord in the beauty of holiness" (Ps. 96:9, KJV) because to him belongs "The greatness, and the power, and the glory, and the victory, and the majesty: for all that is in the heavens and in the earth is thine . . . and thou art exalted as head above all" (I Chron. 29:11).

* * *

There came a time, Luke tells us in the eleventh chapter of his Gospel, when the disciples realized their poverty in the area of prayer. They came to Jesus asking, "Lord, teach us to pray" (v. 1). There may even have been some jealousy present, for they noted that the disciples of John the Baptist had

118

learned a prayer. What Jesus gave them was a re-markable piece of set liturgy, to be memorized and used over and over again. It encompassed acknowledgment of God's holiness, authority, majesty, and graciousness. It confessed man's failure, his need both to forgive and to be forgiven, and his total dependence on God, even for everyday needs. And it included the petition to see the Kingdom of Heaven reflected here on earth. Its comprehensiveness was all the more startling for its brevity. It has come to be known as the Lord's Prayer. This piece of set liturgy was Christ's response to his disciples' need. The Anglican liturgy can be another answer to man's quest for communication with God.

Questions for Thought and Discussion

1. Do you agree with the attitude of the early church that "those who have not yet put on Christ cannot join in offering prayer"?

2. Is a set liturgy meaningful to you? Is the Anglican church's solution of including both the traditional and contemporary services in the same book a viable solution to the controversy over set or free prayers? What are the benefits and detriments of both types of services?

3. What is the key to true worship? Is it really important whether the liturgy—the work of the people—be set or extemporaneous?

10

Rites and Ceremonies

AS OUR EARLIER DISCUSSION of the Oxford Movement suggested, the question of what is proper ceremonial has long divided Anglicans. As early as the first prayer book of Edward VI (1549), Archbishop Cranmer thought it necessary to include a lengthy rubric entitled "Of Ceremonies, Why Some Be Abolished and Some Retained." His reason for stripping away much of the accumulated practice of the Middle Ages was that the gospel is not a ceremonial law. In sharp contrast to the numerous ritual ordinances in Judaism, the New Testament says little about the external manner for worshiping God, except that it must be done "decently and in order" (I Cor. 14:40).

Cranmer wanted certain medieval ceremonies "put away" for two reasons. First, the sheer complexity of ritual had become an intolerable burden.

Ceremony had been added to ceremony until at last there was "an excessive multitude of ceremonies." If Augustine had complained of too much ritual, "What would he have said if he had seen the ceremonies used among us, whereunto the multitude used in his time was not to be compared?" This extensive ritual simply confused and darkened people's understanding of the gospel.

Secondly, and far worse in Cranmer's opinion, was the interpretation attached to this ceremony. Though certain practices had begun with godly intent and purpose, too many had turned into vanity and superstition. Other rituals were introduced that had no legitimate biblical basis at all. Though "they were winked at in the beginning they grew daily to more and more abuses, which not only for their unprofitableness, but also because they . . . obscured the glory of God, are worthy to be cut away and clean rejected." When ceremonial ceases to draw reverent attention to Christ and begins calling attention to itself or anything else, it is to be abolished.

As we can infer from our brief study of the Articles of Religion, the superstition surrounding the elements of the Communion service was of particular concern to the Reformers. If people believed in transubstantiation and thought the bread and wine actually became Christ's body and blood, it would follow that the elements themselves should be the focus of worship. This was in fact the case, and a great deal of medieval piety was directed to the sacrament: bowing to it, praying to it, and worshiping it outright. According to Article 28 this was all to cease: "The Sacrament of the Lord's Supper was not by Christ's ordinance reserved, carried about, lifted up, or worshiped."

There was a similar protest leveled by the Reformers against the practice of praying to the saints and to their statues and relics. This too had come to dominate medieval worship. Dr. Philip Hughes emphasized in his *Theology of the English Reformers* "that in the Litany . . . all invocations addressed to the Virgin Mary, angels, and saints—so characteristic of unreformed worship—were completely removed. Throughout the length of the Prayer Book all prayers are offered to God through Jesus Christ, and through no other mediator."[29]

Significantly, Cranmer did not call for the complete abolition of all ceremonial. He recognized that anything that is done corporately must have some guidelines: "Without some ceremonies it is not possible to keep any order or quiet discipline in the church." Indeed, Article 34 cautions against doing away with those traditions and ceremonies that are not "repugnant to the Word of God." The guidelines Cranmer used to decide which ceremonies would remain were:

- They must mediate the gospel responsibly.
- They must be explained clearly, so that everyone could understand what they mean.

● They must never be confused in their importance with the unchanging truth of God's Word.

Ceremonies come and go. By their very nature they may be altered and changed. But, Cranmer said, it "is no small offence" to trample on tradition just for the sake of novelty. The concern of the English Reformers was not to satisfy either the traditionalists or the innovators but to please God.

A study of the history of ritual leads to some remarkable conclusions. The first is that many revered traditions are at best arbitrary; they may even be accidental! Many things were originally done for one reason, which are now justified and explained on different grounds.

The original purpose of candles, for instance, was obviously to give light. But over the years various symbolic explanations have been attached to them. For instance, it is said that the two Communion candles are there to represent Christ's two natures. By now, it seems unthinkable to many people that there could be a proper service without candles. It would appear a denial of the person of Christ, however little they might be needed for illumination.

For the first eight or nine centuries of Christian history, organs were not used in worship, though they had been in existence since the third century B.C. It was thought that since Scripture did not mention organs, they were inappropriate or pagan. Today there are those who seem unable to appreciate any form of church music *but* the organ. Many are offended by the use of a guitar, even though it is far more biblical as a stringed instrument.

The clergyman's collar is said to be symbolic of his being yoked to Christ. Originally, it was the same collar worn by any Victorian gentleman, turned backward because the necktie was considered ostentatious.

Following the breaking of the bread, a priest typically brings his thumb and forefinger together, forming a circle on each hand. This is said to be symbolic of the Trinity. Actually, it comes from a rather excessive concern that fingers which have touched the Blessed Sacrament not touch anything else.

The ablutions or washing of the hands and communion vessels during the service derive from this same concern. We find ablutions being performed nearly everywhere in Anglicanism today, even where transubstantiation is the farthest thing from anyone's mind.

We see the same carry-over in the widespread practice of bowing and genuflecting. For whatever reasons people think they bow today, it was originally a form of devotion to the body and blood of Christ, literally present because of the alleged miracle of transubstantiation.

Lifting up or elevating the elements is often thought to symbolize offering them to the people. Historically, it was a matter of offering them to God, precisely as a sacrifice. This was so clearly the understanding that the Reformers forbade the gesture altogether.

The Roman Catholic practice of giving only the bread to the laity began with the fear that laymen might spill the wine. If they dropped the bread, it could be recovered; if they spilled the wine, it was lost forever. Since it was thought to be Christ's precious blood, that was too great a risk. Rather remarkably, Anglican tradition has partly reversed this distinction. In our church, licensed laymen are permitted to distribute the cup but not the bread; and they may read the Epistle but not the Gospel (except at morning and evening prayer, when it is perfectly legitimate!).

A friend tells the delightful story of the "Church of the Holy Radiator." It seems that in a particular parish, it was the rector's custom to lift the chalice ever-so-reverently to just touch an exposed radiator pipe in the sanctuary. Only then would he offer the wine to his people. Apparently, most of them were certain this had deep theological significance; they were offended when a visiting clergyman failed to do this. Actually, the rector walked with a limp, and as he shuffled his feet across the carpet, he built up a considerable charge of static electricity. His radiator ritual was simply to discharge it!

It should only be added that traditions have begun with far less cause than that.

It seems quite safe to say that there is no such thing as pure ceremony. The liturgical practice of any given parish or clergyman combines a bit of this and that from many different periods in the life of the church. Specific local needs and preferences have dictated "proper ceremony" as much as long-standing traditions. Even the great classic rites of Christian antiquity (the Roman rite, the Sarum rite, etc.) have been infiltrated (to use Dix's word[30]) by various eccentricities. The order in which prayers occur, their specific phrases, the hymns and canticles that surround them, all have been almost totally rearranged in the course of two millennia. If that is true of the words, how much more so the actions that accompany them.

While it is possible to find a reason for doing nearly anything, that reason may be merely a rationalization. There are at least two questions here: whether or not a thing may be done and whether or not it should be done. The first asks whether there is any conceivable justification for a given ritual. (There almost surely will be.) But the second presses the issue: is this particular ritual so liable to possible misinterpretation that it would be better to drop it altogether? Thus, many evangelicals have given up the practice of bowing and genuflecting, even though they recognize that this can be justified, with a little work.

What needs to be realized is that to insist "this is the only way to do things" is almost always false, both historically and theologically.

Take liturgical color as an example. In the English

tradition alone, nearly every conceivable variation of color sequence has been tried between the 1200s and the present time. At one point, the color for Lent was black. At another, it was blue. At another, unbleached white or gray. At still another, violet. A good reason can be given for using any of these colors. White is the symbol of Christ's purity, black the symbol of his approaching death, blue or violet the symbol of our penitence. But that demonstrates that no one of them is beyond contention.

Somehow we need to strike a balance. Yes, of course it matters (everything matters in our worship of God!), and on the other hand, it does not matter absolutely.

Churches have been torn by allowing such secondary concerns to become more important than they ought to be. Shall we dress the choir in traditional vestments or in contemporary robes? Should the bishop wear a cope and mitre or only a chimere and rochet? Should the acolytes bow every time they move across the sanctuary or only upon entering and leaving it? Should the clergy make the sign of the cross with three fingers, with the open hand, or not at all?

Do we really think God cares? And if he doesn't, why do we?

We come to a final comment: what is reverence to one man is sometimes idolatry to another. There are those whose most minimal expression of reverence is to bow their heads as the processional cross comes down the aisle. They are not worshiping the cross. They are worshiping the One who died there for the forgiveness of their sins. But there are others for whom that same cross symbolizes the persecution of protestants and evangelicals in places like South America. When they see a cross leading a procession, something inside them turns cold and hard. Still others think bowing as the cross enters is bowing before a graven image. They would sooner die.

One of the great strengths of the Anglican church is that it makes no such demands. Compared with most other Protestant denominations, Anglicanism has a great wealth of ritual and ceremonial. But it has very few requirements regarding them. The individual is free to express his love of God as he sees fit. Cranmer states in his rubric that ''touching, kneeling, crossing, holding up hands, knocking upon the breast, and other gestures; they may be used or left as every man's devotion serves without blame.''

* * *

Saint Paul's letter to the Romans reveals that even then Christians criticized each other. Apparently some still preferred Saturday as the day for worship, as had been the Jewish practice. Others were already observing Sunday, the day of the Resurrection. Some were vegetarians; others saw nothing wrong with eating meat. Paul had strong words for these critical Christians. ''Who are you to pass judgment on the servant of another? It is before his own master that he stands or falls'' (Rom. 14:4).

God is the only one who sees our hearts, and only he can rightly evaluate the quality of our worship. "Let us no more pass judgment on one another," said Paul, "but rather decide never to put a stumbling block or hindrance in the way of a brother." Do not, for the sake of externals, "destroy the work of God" (Rom. 14:13, 20). Of course, ceremony matters, but it does not matter absolutely.

Questions for Thought and Discussion

1. Do you agree with Cranmer's reasons for reforming medieval ceremonial? Might some of these reasons still apply to ceremonies today? Could the guidelines Cranmer suggested to evaluate ceremonial be used today?

2. The author states that many revered traditions and ceremonies are at best arbitrary. Are there some ceremonies that aren't?

3. Is the standard the author sets for evaluating a ceremony (whether it will be misinterpreted) valid? Can you think of other standards beside this and Cranmer's?

4. What were some of the criticisms that Christians in Rome made of one another? (See the Book of Romans.) What did Paul say their attitude should be regarding these differences? Are there any specific arguments like these in your church? What can you do to bring about reconciliation?

11

The Lord's Supper

This is my body which is given for you. Do this in
remembrance of me. . . . This cup is the new covenant
in my blood. Do this, as often as you drink it, in
remembrance of me (I Cor. 11:24, 25).

What did Jesus possibly mean? As we return again
and again to the subject of Holy Communion, we see
that this is one of the most important questions that
has ever been asked. Our word *communion* means
common union; yet the Lord's Supper has caused
violent discord among Christ's followers. Dis-
agreement over what it is and what it means has led
one group of Christians to break away from another
time and time again.

There was a good deal of change in the practice of
Holy Communion within the New Testament itself.
The Lord's Supper was originally just that—a supper

or meal. Jesus broke the bread in the context of a Passover meal, a celebration that was already highly stylized and heavy with symbolism. Every element in the meal recalled the miraculous deliverance of the ancient Israelites from cruel slavery in Egypt. Lamb was the main course, commemorating the lamb's blood splashed on the doorway of Israelite homes so the angel of death would pass over. Bitter herbs reminded the Jews of the bitterness of their bondage. A paste of mashed fruits and nuts symbolized the bricks the Israelites had been forced to make for Pharaoh. And—especially—there was bread. Passover was called the feast of unleavened bread. Leaven or yeast was always a symbol of corruption to the Jews, and this very special Passover bread was to have no leaven in it. It symbolized the purity of Israel, redeemed by God's grace. Finally, there was wine, a symbol of life and blessing.

It was in the midst of celebrating that meal that Jesus took first the bread and later the wine, gave thanks for them, identified them with his own body and blood, and distributed them with the words "Do this in remembrance of me."

The bread and wine, which already symbolized Israel's deliverance from the corruption of Egypt, were now to have a new meaning as well. They were to signify Christ's body and blood, about to be broken and poured out to deliver us from the corruption of sin. And he said, "Do this."

But do what? Eat and drink in remembrance; let

your very eating and drinking be a vivid recollection of Christ. His disciples might have understood him to mean that the *Passover* bread and wine were to be consumed in remembrance of him. Certainly he meant that much! But they took a broader interpretation: *whenever* Christians gather to eat and drink together, it is to be in remembrance of Christ.

The Book of Acts records that over three thousand people were converted at the first preaching of the gospel on the day of Pentecost. These earliest converts "devoted themselves to the apostles' teaching and fellowship, to the breaking of bread and the prayers" (Acts 2:42). Then, as now, the "breaking of bread" meant two things: an ordinary meal and the celebration of the Lord's Supper. At the outset of Christian history, however, these two things were one and the same.

The Scripture continues, "All who believed were together and had all things in common. . . . And day by day, attending the temple together and breaking bread in their homes, they partook of food with glad and generous hearts" (Acts 2:44-47). Professor G. H. C. Macgregor writes in *The Interpreter's Bible,* "The close conjunction in vs. 46 of *breaking bread* and *they partook of food* proves that the former, though already of religious significance, was still part of a regular nourishing meal. . . . It was only later that the Eucharist [Holy Communion] became differentiated from the agape [fellowship meal]."[31]

We see, then, that the earliest communion services were in the homes of Christians on a daily basis as people held open house to their fellow believers. (Obviously, three thousand people could not easily assemble for meals in any single place every day.) These first communion services must have resembled a potluck supper more than a typical church service. Significantly, for about a hundred years, it was common to share the Supper of the Lord in this way, without insisting that a presbyter-bishop preside or even be present.

However, even in that first generation of Christians, problems developed that led to a tremendous change in the character of the Lord's Supper. Paul wrote to the Corinthians, "When you meet together, it is not the Lord's supper that you eat. For in eating, each one goes ahead with his own meal, and one is hungry and another is drunk. What! Do you not have houses to eat and drink in?" (I Cor. 11:20-22).

Just as Ananias and Sapphira held back some of their possessions (Acts 5), so the Christians in Corinth were coming to the Communion supper with no intention of sharing their food. Some came and overindulged—even to the point of gluttony and drunkenness—while others went hungry. This was a denial of common union, and Paul said it would be better to eat separately in their own homes rather than make a mockery of coming together.

He continued, "When you come together to eat, wait for one another—if anyone is hungry, let him eat at home—lest you come together to be condemned'' (I Cor. 11:33, 34). The potluck supper had been so abused that it was to be discontinued. People were to eat in their own homes before gathering with the rest of the local church. The Lord's Supper, having been part of a real meal, was from now on to be strictly symbolic. Instead of eating and drinking for nourishment, people were now to partake just a small amount: a single mouthful of bread, a sip of wine.

It was in the very middle of this whole discussion that Paul made the extremely strong statement that ''Whoever, therefore, eats the bread or drinks the cup of the Lord in an unworthy manner will be guilty of profaning the body and blood of the Lord. Let a man examine himself, and so eat of the bread and drink of the cup. For anyone who eats and drinks without discerning the body eats and drinks judgment upon himself'' (I Cor. 11:27-29).

Does discerning the body mean perceiving that the bread has become Christ's literal flesh? Nothing could have been farther from Paul's mind. ''The body'' is the metaphor he consistently used for our oneness in Christ, a metaphor he developed at great length in the next chapter. The Church is the Body of Christ. To come to Communion and fail to see that in Christ we are made one body, to behave selfishly there of all places, is to eat and drink unworthily. Paul did not, in the midst of discussing Christian manners, introduce a totally extraneous reference to a supernatural transformation of bread into flesh. He

134

consistently developed a single issue and used a particularly common metaphor to illustrate it.

But what of his comment that by their abuse of the Communion meal the Corinthians were actually "profaning the body and blood of the Lord"? Here he simply articulated a principle that runs through the whole of Scripture: to dishonor the symbol of anything is to dishonor the thing itself. Why, for instance, did Samson lose his strength when his hair was cut? Because it was magic hair? No, because it was the symbol of his dedication to the Lord—a dedication that resulted in his unique strength. He despised the symbol and forfeited the reality.

The strong connection between a symbol and the thing it symbolizes is one of the grand themes of the Bible. The Communion meal, eaten in remembrance of Christ, symbolizes both our union with him and each other and his death on our behalf. To profane the elements, the symbols of his body and blood, is to profane the reality behind them. But the symbols should never be mistaken for the reality itself. That would be idolatry.

Perhaps the confusion began when Jesus himself said, "I am the bread of life . . . unless you eat the flesh of the Son of man and drink his blood, you have no life in you; he who eats my flesh and drinks my blood has eternal life, and I will raise him up at the last day" (John 6: 48, 53, 54). These are hard words indeed; but why did anyone ever take them as more than a metaphor, albeit a powerful one?

135

To eat and drink metaphorically is to consume, to feast upon, to be nourished by, to draw one's strength from, to be absolutely dependent upon this living bread, this Jesus. How do we do that? By putting our faith in him. It is a spiritual and metaphorical, not a physical, eating.

Jesus said precisely this in the same passage: "It is the spirit that gives life, the flesh is of no avail; the words that I have spoken to you are spirit and life. But there are some of you that do not believe" (John 6:63, 64). How do we consume Jesus? By devouring his words. By finding all spiritual nourishment in him. By believing.

If Jesus had always spoken literally, that interpretation might be questionable. But he taught in parables. He loved symbolism. He called himself the Good Shepherd; the Door; the Light of the World; the Way; the Truth; the Life; the Sower of good seed; the Stone which the builders rejected; the Rock on which to build; the Resurrection; the True Vine; the Bridegroom. He called his body a temple. When John the Baptist called him the Lamb of God, he accepted it.

Why out of all these symbols did people begin to take the one reference to flesh and blood literally?

In his massive *History of Dogma*, Adolph Harnack gives us the answer. In the third century when the state began to impose Christianity on multitudes of pagans, tremendous accommodations had to be made to their deeply ingrained beliefs and practices.

136

The worship of many Greek and Roman gods was transferred to Christian saints. Wherever possible, the heathen mysteries were incorporated into Christian worship. The Christian presbyterate was remodeled after the pagan priesthood. As a consequence, says Harnack,

> the idea crept in that the body and blood of Christ were constantly offered to God afresh in order to propitiate him. . . . The desire for a sensuous expiatory sacrifice, which had been present, though in a hidden form, at an early date, became stronger and stronger, and thus "flesh and blood"—namely, the flesh and blood of Christ—were described as sacrificial offerings. Thus men had once more a bloody sacrifice . . . and what it seemed not to have certainly accomplished when offered once, was to be accomplished by a repetition of it . . . *It was nothing but pure Paganism which had brought this about.*[32]

Increasingly, the theologians of the third century, particularly Cyprian of Carthage (200-258), reinterpreted the ministry and worship of Christianity in the light of the surrounding culture. They found biblical grounds for doing so by viewing the New Testament through the perspective of the Old, an exact reversal of what the Book of Hebrews says should have happened. Thus, not only pagan sacrifice but also the whole system of Jewish sacrifice with its Levitical priesthood was superimposed on the Holy Communion. Harnack writes, "It must have been of the most wide-reaching significance, that a wealth of ideas was in this way connected with the ordinance [of the Lord's Supper], which had nothing whatever in common either with the purpose of the meal as a memorial of Christ's death, or with the mysterious symbols of the body and blood of Christ."[33] Prior to this there were suggestions of such an interpretation, but only now did it begin to crystalize. But it was still a very long way from becoming official dogma.

Nearly five hundred years later in the middle of the ninth century, a monk named Radbertus from the monastery of Corbie set down the first thoroughgoing treatise on the Lord's Supper. Radbertus taught that "by divine miracle the substance of the elements is made the very body and blood of Christ."[34] Here is the real beginning of the doctrine later known as transubstantiation. But the word itself was not coined until the eleventh century.

We must not miss the significance of Radbertus' position. Harnack comments, *"For the first time in the Church he declares without hesitancy that the sacramental body is that which had been born of Mary, and that this is due to a transformation which only leaves the sensuous appearance unchanged."*[35] It took eight hundred years to come up with the full-blown idea of transubstantiation, and it would be still another four centuries before the doctrine was officially accepted by the Roman Catholic church.

In 1049 the head of the cathedral school in Tours,

a theologian named Berengar, denied that the substance of bread and wine actually changed. Instead, he argued, "something invisible but real is added to the natural elements, namely the whole heavenly Christ."[36] This was roughly what came to be known later as the doctrine of the real presence. But Berengar's position was not strong enough to suit his superior, Cardinal Humbert. Humbert forced him to sign a statement to the effect that "at the communion the priest touches the body and blood of Christ and that the communicants bite into the Lord's body with their teeth."[37]

The whole controversy continued until in 1215 the Fourth Lateran Council ruled in favor of transubstantiation and settled the matter for the Roman church. Thomas Aquinas had refined and elaborated the doctrine, and it had been reaffirmed by other theologians and councils; but it was the early 1200s before it was cast in its classic medieval form.

We have already seen that this view led to the adoration and worship of the sacramental elements and to the belief that here—especially—grace was dispensed. The transubstantiation of the bread and wine meant that Christ's body and blood were literally in the hands of the priest on the altar of the church. Increasingly, one's whole relationship to God focused on coming and eating, not metaphorically, not spiritually, but physically.

We have also seen that one of the major themes of the English Reformation was the complete denial of this heresy. Archbishop Cranmer in his *Answer to Gardiner* said, ''They (the Romanists) say that Christ is corporally (physically) under or in the form of bread and wine; *we say that Christ is not there, neither corporally nor spiritually.*'' [38]

Bishop Hooper reaffirmed this belief when he stated, ''I do not believe that the Body of Christ can be contained, hid, or enclosed in the bread, under the bread, or with the bread—neither the blood in the wine, under the wine, or with the wine.''[39]

Bishop Ridley in his *Disputation at Oxford* also interpreted the words ''This is my body'' to have ''a figurative sense and meaning.''[40] And Richard Hooker said, ''The real presence of Christ's most blessed body and blood is not to be sought for in the sacrament, but in the worthy receiver of the sacrament.''[41] Such statements could be multiplied almost endlessly.

What then does the Anglican church believe and teach concerning the Lord's Supper? Its official position is precisely what Jesus himself taught, precisely what the New Testament and the apostolic church believed and taught:

- That Christ is surely present in the celebration of his Supper, but in the hearts of believers and in their faithful reception of the elements of bread and wine, not in the elements themselves.
- That his death on the cross was ''a full, perfect, and sufficient sacrifice, oblation and satisfaction

for the sins of the whole world'' (Prayer of Consecration). We neither add to it nor repeat it. The only sacrifice we make is the offering of our praise and thanksgiving to God.

• That the physical bread and wine remain unchanged, but in being consecrated or set aside for a holy purpose, they become a powerful metaphor. Just as we consume them physically with our mouths, so we are nourished by Christ spiritually by faith.

• That our Communion is a common union. As we participate in the Lord's Supper, we are assured of our membership in ''the mystical body'' of Christ, ''which is the blessed company of all faithful people.''

The strong bond between the symbol and the thing symbolized is rehearsed over and over in the Communion prayers. We ask that ''we and all others who shall be partakers of this Holy Communion, may worthily receive the most precious Body and Blood of thy Son Jesus Christ, and to drink his blood'' that we may be cleansed and dwell in him—intending the figurative meaning that Christ gave these words. We take and eat the bread literally in our mouths ''in remembrance that Christ died'' for us, and we ''feed upon him'' spiritually, in our ''hearts, by faith, with thanksgiving.'' We drink literal wine ''in remembrance that Christ's Blood was shed'' for us. And finally, we give thanks to God that as we have ''duly received these holy mysteries" of bread and wine, he has also fed us "with the spiritual food of the most precious Body and Blood" of his Son our Saviour. We thus proclaim his death by our celebration.

* * *

Jesus once compared his crucifixion to an incident in the ministry of Moses. The Israelites were complaining against God, and "the Lord sent fiery serpents among the people" and many died from their bites. When Moses begged God for relief, the Lord instructed him to make a serpent of bronze and put it on a pole. When those who were bitten looked on the serpent, they lived (Num. 21: 4-9).

Jesus said that he also would be lifted up on the cross, that whoever believed in him might have eternal life (John 3: 14, 15). The bread and wine symbolizes our deliverance by Christ's death just as the bronze serpent symbolized God's deliverance from snakebite.

But some of us have become as confused as the Israelites did. For six hundred years after Moses made the bronze serpent, it was *worshiped* by the people! The people of Israel confused symbol with reality. Not until Hezekiah inherited the throne of Israel was the bronze serpent broken into pieces as an abomination to the Lord (2 Kings 18).

Questions for Thought and Discussion

1. How does the Israelites' perspective of bread,

wine, and the Passover meal add to the meaning of Holy Communion?

2. What did Christ intend Holy Communion to be? Why would he feel such a service was necessary?

3. How would you describe the relationship between symbol and reality as the Bible uses these concepts?

4. In what sense does the Anglican church teach that Christ is present in the Communion service? Have you felt his presence there?

5. What do we express about our relationship with Christ when we participate in Holy Communion? About our relationship with each other?

12

Baptism and Confirmation

SINCE THE TIME of the Reformation at least, the subject of baptism has been nearly as controversial as the Lord's Supper. The question of baptizing infants has been of particular concern. What is baptism? Is it a request that God would grant salvation or a recognition that he has done so? If a person already believes in Christ, what does baptism add? If he doesn't, how can it help? Why do we baptize those who are too young to intelligently believe in Christ or even understand what is happening to them? Does the Anglican church teach that because someone was baptized as a child, he has no need to be converted? How can that be reconciled with Jesus' statement that "unless one is born anew, he cannot see the kingdom of God" (John 3:3)? Does baptism confer the new birth? If it does, why are there so many apparently "dead" Christians? If it does not, how dare we say in the baptismal service that "this Child is regenerate"?

As we have already seen, these questions were among the issues that led to the breaking away of the Reformed Episcopal Church in America a century ago. They are being thrust upon us with fresh urgency today as throughout the world Anglicans are again recognizing the high priority of evangelism. How do we relate this call to commitment or conversion to our traditional practice of baptizing children?

We need to realize that baptism was a well-established Jewish practice long before it took on its specifically Christian meaning. Somewhere along the way—no one knows just when—the Jews adopted the custom of requiring that outsiders who wanted to become Jewish be baptized to wash away their sinful past. It is somewhat odd that they did this, since God had given them the initiation rite of circumcision. Perhaps they adopted baptism, which was common among religions of the ancient world, because its symbolism was so much more obvious than that of circumcision. It was also a good deal less painful and applicable to women as well as men.

In any event, for at least two hundred years before Christ, Jews insisted that their Gentile converts be baptized. While this ceremony brought outsiders into Judaism, it also clearly marked them as different from those who had been born Jewish. The Jews themselves were never baptized. They were already children of Abraham and heirs of the Covenant.

They gloried in their heritage and felt no need to wash away their past.

This helps us appreciate the impact of John the Baptist's ministry, for he burst upon the scene with the devastating proclamation that the Jews did *not* have an inside track to God. They too had a sinful past; they also needed to be washed. "Repent and be baptized," shouted John, "or face God's anger."

But John introduced an even more important element than that. "Get ready," he said. "There is one coming who is mightier than I . . . who will baptize you with the Holy Spirit and with fire" (Luke 3:16). Baptism had been a symbol of external change or repentance. It was to become a symbol of internal transformation as well. The real baptism, the crucial one, was yet to come. It would be a baptism not with water but with the Holy Spirit. Just as John drenched people with water, so there was one coming who would literally saturate them with the Holy Spirit. Shortly that One appeared and asked to be baptized.

John's first response was to protest: "I need to be baptized by you, and do you come to me?" (Matt. 3:14). But Jesus insisted that it was appropriate for him to participate in the ritual cleansing to identify himself with those who needed washing. But, in the very midst of that identification, God declared him different: "This is my beloved Son, with whom I am well pleased" (Matt. 3:17). They were sinners who needed God's pardon; he was the beloved Son who evoked God's pleasure.

With that pronouncement, the Spirit of God descended like a dove, empowering Jesus for service. The one who was to baptize others was so baptized at the outset of his public ministry.

John's ministry marked a transition from Jewish baptism to Christian baptism in two regards. First, it anticipated the time when water baptism would be an external symbol not just of repentance but of baptism with the Holy Spirit. Secondly, it became the vehicle for Jesus' identification with sinners, and they with him.

Jesus then added another critical dimension to baptism by asking his disciples, "Are you able to drink the cup that I drink, or to be baptized with the baptism with which I am baptized?" (Mark 10:38). The ominous double reference was to his impending crucifixion. It becomes apparent that Jesus saw in baptism the same symbolism of death and burial that Paul was later to elaborate in his letter to the Romans. "We were buried therefore with him," said Paul, "by baptism into death, so that as Christ was raised from the dead by the glory of the Father, we too might walk in newness of life" (Rom. 6:4).

The symbolism here is much more vivid if we think of baptism by total immersion, although Scripture doesn't insist it be done that way. The baptismal candidate "dies" as by drowning and is totally "buried" not with earth but with water. But then he rises again from his watery grave by the power of God; it is a resurrection!

It can hardly be accidental that as Jesus anticipated his death, he described it in the symbolic terms of both of the sacraments he left us to commemorate it. "The cup that I drink" is recalled in every Communion service. The baptism of death and burial is dramatized in Christian initiation. Thus we see that both of these sacraments mean essentially the same thing. Both symbolize and recall the death of Christ on our behalf and our identification with him by faith. The difference is that baptism happens once and is not to be repeated. The Communion service is repeated over and over again, and with each celebration, we reaffirm our baptismal experience.

As we see the close connection between these two sacraments, we can anticipate our next discovery. As the church moved farther and farther from a clear biblical basis, its reinterpretation of the Lord's Supper was paralleled by a reinterpretation of baptism. Christ gave the bread and wine to symbolize his flesh and blood; in Roman theology, they became his flesh and blood. Water baptism was to symbolize the baptism of the Holy Spirit; in Roman theology, it became the baptism of the Spirit. Rather than symbolizing the washing away of our sins by repentance and faith, baptism became the washing itself. It was said that whatever sins had been committed before baptism were completely dissolved by it. People actually delayed their baptism as long as they dared, hoping to receive full pardon on their deathbeds and avoid purgatory—a tricky business indeed!

It was this interpretation that so greatly confused the matter. As early as the middle of the second century, teachers such as Hermas of Rome and Justin Martyr had all but obliterated the distinction between symbol and reality.[42] To be baptized with water was to be baptized with or to receive the Holy Spirit—to be born again by the power of God.

That the New Testament does not teach this is very clear. It consistently distinguishes between rebirth itself and baptism as a symbol of it. The New Testament uses several terms interchangeably such as being reborn, becoming regenerate, becoming a child of God, and receiving the Spirit. But its typical pattern was that people were first reborn—or converted and *then* baptized in water as a public demonstration of their faith. The experience of Cornelius and his family is an example. Cornelius, a centurion, was a Gentile, and there was considerable question in the minds of Jewish Christians as to whether he could join them. But Peter's witness was, "As I began to speak [proclaiming the gospel], the Holy Spirit fell on them just as on us at the beginning. And I remembered the word of the Lord, how he said, 'John baptized with water, but you shall be baptized with the Holy Spirit.' If then God gave the same gift to them as he gave to us when we believed in the Lord Jesus Christ, who was I that could withstand God?" (Acts 11:15-17) Thus, Cornelius and his family, having already been born again or baptized in the Spirit, were baptized in water and admitted to the church. The one thing symbolized the other.

But this brings us back to the question of infant baptism. What does a believer do about his family? What is the status of a believer's children? What did Peter mean when he spoke of Cornelius's household being saved (Acts 11:14)? This was a very common phrase in the New Testament. Paul told the frightened jailer in Philippi, "Believe in the Lord Jesus, and you will be saved, you and your household . . . and he was baptized at once, with all his family" (Acts 16:31-33). Lydia, the seller of purple goods, believed, and "she was baptized with her household" (Acts 16:15). We read that "Crispus, the ruler of the synagogue, believed in the Lord, together with all his household . . . and [along with many others, they] were baptized" (Acts 18:8). Paul wrote to the Corinthians, "I did baptize also the household of Stephanas" (I Cor. 1:16).

Professor Stauffer's careful study of the term *household* demonstrates that in biblical usage it meant an extended family: several generations living together and often the families of servants as well. Stauffer comments that *household* included "not simply the children in addition to the adults, but the children *quite especially,* and not least any *little children* who might be present."[43]

The case becomes even stronger when we recall again that baptism was a well-established rite of initiation long before Jesus gave it Christian significance. Both in the Hellenistic environment and in

Judaism particularly, children and babies were always included in baptism when Gentiles converted.[44] The Jews included their own sons in the rite of circumcision when they were only eight days old.

This had nothing to do with automatic or mechanical grace. It was the simple recognition that God deals with people through their families as well as individuals. The Jewish baby who was circumcised, the Gentile baby baptized with his family into Judaism, both had to come into a living personal faith of their own, or the ceremony availed them nothing.

This seems to be the perspective carried into the New Testament. Peter's first sermon on the day of Pentecost declared that "the promise is to you and to your children" (Acts 2:39). In no way does that minimize a child's need to be converted. But it does take seriously God's promise to draw our children to himself as we do our part in raising them according to his standards.

"Train up a child in the way he should go, and when he is old he will not depart from it," promises the Scripture (Prov. 22:6). Does that mean sending him to an hour of church school each week? The Book of Deuteronomy suggests something a bit more strenuous: "These words which I command you this day shall be upon your heart; and you shall teach them diligently to your children, and shall talk of them when you sit in your house, and when you walk by the way, and when you lie down, and when you rise. . . . you and your son and your son's son by keeping all his statutes and commandments . . . that it may go well with you'' (Deut. 6:2, 3, 6, 7, 18). Believing parents are not only to insist on God's standards; they are to enforce their insistence with "the rod of discipline" (Prov. 22:15). They are not to abuse their authority, of course, but in love they are to bring up their children "in the discipline and instruction of the Lord" (Eph. 6:4). As they do so, they may reasonably expect that he will keep them as his own and bring them into a mature faith.

This, then, would seem to be the New Testament view of child rearing and the rational for baptizing infants. It was surely the view of the English Reformers, who knew nothing more of automatic grace in baptism than they did in the Lord's Supper.

Archbishop Cranmer said flatly, "Not all that are washed with water are washed with the Holy Spirit.''[45] Bishop Hugh Latimer wrote, "Christ said, 'Except a man be born again from above, he cannot see the kingdom of God.' Ye must have a Regeneration: and what is this Regeneration? It is not to be christened in water as these firebrands [the Roman Catholics] expound it, and nothing else.''[46] Similar statements could again be added endlessly.

Thus we see that to pronounce that a child is regenerate is simply to include him in the promise. But, just as one can eat and drink judgment to himself in the Communion service, one can deny his baptism by faithlessness and unbelief. The church

152

has witnessed the sorry spectacle of children being brought for baptism whose parents and sponsors have no genuine faith of their own and neither the intention nor the ability to fulfill their part of the bargain with God. Are we really surprised that the children fail to grow up as converted Christians? We need to be much more careful about instructing people as to the meaning and responsibilities of baptism.

Let us insist on classes for parents and sponsors who want their children baptized. Some may well reconsider their readiness to accept such responsibility, but others might find their own Christian experience growing and deepening as they better appreciate what is involved in sponsoring their children. One of the most exciting moments in a pastor's life comes when parents who had planned to baptize their child simply because it was expected suddenly discover what a living, vital relationship with Christ is all about and ask him into *their* lives.

Finally, it was precisely the recognition that the baptism of an infant would have to be ratified as he grew up that gave rise to the discipline of confirmation. In the apostolic age, baptism was usually accompanied by the laying on of hands and sometimes by anointing with oil as well. But the two things gradually became separated as the church looked for an appropriate way to symbolize the adult commitment of those who had been baptized as infants. Former Presiding Bishop John Hines wrote that the specific rite of confirmation grew out of ceremonies "designed to prepare the adolescent for the future struggle against the forces of evil. Later feeling was that as one entered the years in which life became increasingly difficult there was a definite need to renew vows and to make that public."[47]

Since the Middle Ages, confirmation has been a prerequisite for receiving the Holy Communion. But increasingly, Episcopal and Anglican churches are reverting to the practice of the early Christians and allowing children to receive Communion prior to confirmation (but following adequate instruction, we hope!). Confirmation then occurs later when it can be an expression of a more thoughtful and mature commitment to Christ. As Bishop Hines suggests, "The responsibility and commitment at baptism are really with the sponsors and the congregation. . . . What Confirmation can be is the opportunity for the baptized member to enter into a concrete covenant, a real commitment."[48]

And that is just the point. Baptism may itself be an expression of a real commitment if one has never been baptized and is converted as an adult. But if one has been raised in a Christian home, was baptized as an infant, and becomes converted as a result of his upbringing, then he will want to confirm in his own name the vows made in his behalf.

* * *

When Paul realized that his own life was likely to end in martyrdom, he wrote to a young man named

Timothy and entrusted a good deal of his responsibility to him. He said, "I am reminded of your sincere faith, a faith that dwelt first in your grandmother Lois and your mother Eunice and now, I am sure, dwells in you" (2 Tim. 1:5). Paul attributed Timothy's spiritual stature partially to the godly beginnings in his home. But he had to make his own "confession in the presence of many witnesses" (I Tim. 6:12). And he received a spiritual gift, Paul said, "through the laying on of my hands" (2 Tim. 1:6). We can get started in the Christian life without our parents' help, but it is a lot harder. Either way, there comes a time when we must make it our own.

Questions for Thought and Discussion

1. Why did John the Baptist say the Jews must repent and be baptized? Do his reasons apply to Christian baptism?

2. What dimensions did Jesus add to the Jewish concept of baptism? What is the relationship between baptism and regeneration?

3. How are baptism and Holy Communion similar? How would these similarities leave both open to revision during the Middle Ages?

4. What do you think the meaning of baptism is? Of confirmation? Are you comfortable with the current trend of allowing children to receive Communion before confirmation and leaving confirmation

to a later time?

5. Why are baptism and confirmation such an important part of a Christian's belief? Why is the controversy over whether baptism is a sign of repentance or an actual receiving of the Holy Spirit important?

6. What reason is there for baptizing babies? Do you think there should be classes for sponsors and parents?

7. What do you think Jesus meant when he said we must "become like little children"? Does this have anything to do with Christians bringing their children to the church for baptism? Is it ever too early for a child to receive and respond to the grace of God? (Luke 1:42) Is it ever too late?

13

The Sleeping Giant Stirs

IN MANY PARTS of the world today, the Anglican church is growing at a phenomenal rate. One African diocese reported nearly twenty thousand confirmations in 1974. In another there were twice that number. The diocese of Sydney, Australia, has more than one million members. In the city of London alone, there are more than a thousand clergymen, eight of them bishops. The current growth rate worldwide is over a million new members each year. The Anglican church has become the fourth largest branch of Christendom (behind the Roman Catholics, Orthodox, and Lutherans), having more than doubled in the last half century.

But in America the Episcopal church has long been known as the "sleeping giant." To a lesser extent, the same is true of the Anglican church in Canada. In spite of its wealth, prestige, the relative social advantage of many of its members, and the heritage it shares with the rest of Anglicanism, the American church is actually shrinking at an alarming rate. The Episcopal church has lost more than half a million members in the last decade.

There are undoubtedly many reasons for this, but the most critical seems to be the neglect of biblical and evangelistic preaching. Rather than proclaiming a gospel that calls for decision, too many Episcopal clergy have assumed that their people have the new life ("After all, they're baptized, aren't they?"); they have spent most of their time talking about Christian ethics and social responsibility. That is like telling a caterpillar to fly. God wants him to, but he needs to get first things first.

Some clergy seem to major in the externals of liturgy and ceremony without knowing much about the cure of souls. Someone has said that is like mistaking the lightning bug for the lightning.

Our Episcopal seminaries must bear a good deal of the blame. Along with many other schools, they have moved away from any real confidence in the authority of Scripture. They have taught liberalism, sacramentalism, and neoorthodoxy, which sees much of the Bible as myth to be demythologized. Many is the graduate who went to seminary to build his faith and lost it there instead. And no one can give to others what he does not have himself.

There are probably other reasons for the decline. Many felt the church should have tried Bishop Pike for his obvious heresy. The church hoped to avoid a scandal of misunderstanding; instead it gave the far more scandalous appearance of endorsing Pike's position as legitimate.

Then the church became involved in a very controversial General Convention Special Program of empowerment (GCSP). Millions of dollars were poured into an attempt to restructure society politically. Though most of the grants were probably very good ones, some funded Marxist and even revolutionary causes. Many Episcopalians protested by withdrawing their money, if not their membership.

Thirdly, the whole business of liturgical reform has been divisive. There is widespread criticism that it was ill considered, poorly timed, and far too drastic.

In these and probably other ways, the Episcopal church has majored in the minors. It has neglected its own heritage. It has broken step with the rest of the Anglican communion. It has not preached conversion. It has not proclaimed the new birth. It has not called men and women to discipleship. It has offered ritualism, traditionalism, liberalism, and even radicalism. But it has declared hesitantly the saving truths of the gospel.

However, a fresh new breeze of the Spirit is beginning to blow through the musty old Episcopal church. Renewal is coming; it is moving in a number of directions. The sleeping giant is beginning to stir.

On Passion Sunday, 1960, the Reverend Dennis

Bennett, then rector of an Episcopal church in California, announced to his parish that he, the wardens, and several other parishioners had received "the baptism of the Holy Spirit." They had not only come into a new and vital relationship with the living Christ, he said, but they had begun to experience some of the dramatic supernatural gifts described in the Book of Acts. They had seen instantaneous healings. They had known answers to prayer. Many of them had begun to speak in tongues—languages they had never studied that enabled them to praise God beyond the limits of English. They felt new joy and a new ability to love.

The announcement was like a bomb blast. One of Bennett's curates threw down his vestments and stormed from the church. Bennett himself was asked to resign—and did so. His bishop issued a pastoral letter banning any "Pentecostal" activity in the diocese, and other bishops joined him. The media picked up the story and sensationalized it. Sides began to be chosen throughout the church.

This event is usually seen as the beginning of neo-Pentecostalism. It was the first time the more controversial gifts of the Spirit had been experienced in a mainline Christian denomination, at least the first publicized time. It remains the most controversial issue in the church today.

The experience spread literally like wildfire through both the Episcopal church and virtually all other branches of Christendom. Dennis Bennett went on to see a tiny mission church in Seattle become a dynamic, exciting, healthy parish—one that not only paid its own way but funded other missions generously.

Other parishes began to grow as they discovered a new quality in Christian fellowship, a new expectancy in worship. Overworked and frustrated rectors found some of their laymen stepping forward to take on responsibilities previously considered the clergy's business. Prayer began to be a thrilling dialogue with God. There were answers to petitions. Some of the sick began to recover. Christians knew God's guidance in their daily lives.

Of course, there were those who wanted nothing to do with this new Pentecostalism. Some were frightened by it; many were confused. Charges were frequently leveled that these charismatics thought themselves superior to other Christians, that they were holier than thou. They were said to divide parishes.

Surely there was an element of truth in these charges, but it takes two to disagree about anything. Pentecostal zealousness has been no more responsible for splitting churches than has resistance to it. The dissension is what Jesus said would happen when new wine was poured into old wineskins.

In his survey of these beginnings, Dr. James Jones has written,

Two points should be kept in mind when considering

161

the neo-Pentecostal movement. First, in its early stages it received a lot of publicity, and this was probably detrimental. It made the participants very self-conscious, and when people are self-conscious they often become defensive and are either unduly aggressive or withdraw into themselves. . . .

Second, many neo-Pentecostals came into the movement with very little knowledge of what it was about. It was often customary for people to be "prayed with" to receive the exercise of spiritual gifts with little prior instruction and no follow-up. . . . There was so little teaching to be had and so few theological resources in their own traditions that they turned increasingly to the classical Pentecostals for instruction.[49]

The classical Pentecostals had begun more than a half century earlier and had positioned themselves in contrast to the major denominations. This needs to be put into perspective. It had been virtually dogma, even among churches that stressed Scripture, that the miraculous events of the New Testament ended with the apostles. But then these Pentecostal Christians began claiming an experience of the supernatural. The mainline churches had to dismiss them as either lunatic or demonic. In the early 1900s, some Pentecostal evangelists were literally tarred and feathered or beaten by their "fellow Christians."

Little wonder it caused a stir when Bennett and scores, then hundreds, then thousands of "perfectly normal people" from traditional churches began sharing such experiences. Integrating them into their backgrounds has hardly been easy.

What has evolved is a great deal of divergent interpretation of the charismatic experience. Some would see it (along with the classical Pentecostals) as a normative "second blessing": a definite, separate outpouring of God's Spirit subsequent to conversion. Others speak of it simply as the fulfillment of the new birth, a coming to fruition of all they were promised in Christ. Still others say it is identical with truly being born again. Many Episcopalians interpret this experience as a fulfillment of what is promised in confirmation.

In the last chapter, we noted that when the New Testament uses the term *baptism of the Spirit,* one of the things it refers to is an empowering for service like the inauguration of Jesus' own ministry. Such an empowering transformed the career of the apostles from a merely human endeavor to a supernatural work of God. We read over and over that they were filled with the Holy Spirit and with power for ministry. The world had to take notice.

Once again the world is taking notice as God is pouring out his Spirit in this present generation. No doubt some of the Pentecostals have been excessive in their claims. For instance, there is nothing in the New Testament to substantiate the statement that all who are filled with the Spirit should speak in tongues. Indeed, the whole point of Paul's discussion of the gifts is just the opposite: God gives us different gifts precisely so we will need each other (I Cor. 12:4-26). It is tragic when one Christian makes another feel inferior because their gifts or experiences are not identical.

But if some of the Pentecostals have been excessively zealous, too many others have been excessively cautious. God is doing a new thing. The wind is blowing, and we are hearing the sound of it. We can argue about where it is coming from and where it is going, but we must not miss Jesus' statement that this is how it is "with everyone who is born of the Spirit" (John 3:8).

In 1973 the Episcopal Charismatic Fellowship came into being at a conference in Dallas. One of its concerns has been to serve the church by consolidating the gains of this new Pentecostalism and placing them firmly on a biblical foundation. With monthly newsletters and frequent regional conferences, great strides have been made in the years of its existence. A number of well-known clergy, from Terry Fullam in Connecticut, to George Stockhowe in Pennsylvania, to Ted Nelson in Texas, to Bishop William Frey in Colorado have joined Dennis Bennett in leading the young movement.

Somewhat related to the fellowship have been a number of dramatic experiments in Christian community. Probably the best known is that of the Church of the Redeemer in Houston. Under the leadership of the Reverend Graham Pulkingham, the members there banded together in "extended families." They shared a common purse, a life-and-death commitment to each other, and a concern to see all the gifts of God's Spirit set free for ministry. Their church went from being a dying inner-city mission to what Ted Holmes of CBS News called "the most exciting and vital example of the new religious way to be found in the country today."[50]

Still, the charismatic movement as a whole is only one of many evidences that God is beginning to shake the giant into wakefulness. The wind is blowing a number of other directions as well.

Laymen throughout the Episcopal church have begun to share their faith with one another and to relate it to the events of daily living. Witnessing Laymen, tutored by Clayton Munroe, Faith Alive! Conferences, under the leadership of Fred Gore, and the Cursillo Movement, which began in the Catholic church, have transformed churches from one end of the country to the other. In all these contexts, Episcopal laymen have shared their faith and experience of Jesus Christ as a living Lord. The results have been contagious.

Other conferences have been sponsored by The Episcopal Center for Evangelism directed by the Reverend Bob Hall and his wife Marjorie. Thousands of people have begun to learn how to present the gospel in simple, clear, and winsome terms to their interested friends.

The Anglican Fellowship of Prayer, founded by the late Dr. Sam Shoemaker and continued until

165

recently by his widow Helen, has helped countless others discover the power of vital prayer. The phrase "Prayer unites" has been proven over and over again as bridges have been built between people of remarkably different backgrounds and temperaments.

The long neglected habit of daily Bible reading is beginning to be reestablished in the homes of many Episcopalians. The Bible Reading Fellowship, under the direction of Harry and Emily Griffith, produces notes and guides for personal devotions and Bible study.

The Fellowship of Witness, led by the Reverend John Guest, is the American branch of the Evangelical Fellowship in the Anglican Communion (EFAC). Concerned to see the Anglican church worldwide return to a thoroughly biblical posture, the Fellowship of Witness sponsors conferences and publishes a quarterly magazine, *Kerygma*. One of the aims of the Fellowship of Witness is "to bear witness with courage and charity to the great Biblical and Reformation principles, so that the Evangelical voice is heard and commended, and an increasing Evangelical contribution made, throughout the Anglican Communion."[51]

Dramatic new life has also been experienced in The Brotherhood of St. Andrew, led by Elmore Hudgens, working among men, and The Daughters of the King, led by Hattie Bunting, working among women.

As the 1973 General Convention approached, an extraordinary thing happened. These several new movements along with a number of others* joined forces in a united front under a banner reading PEWSACTION, which stood for prayer, evangelism, witness, and study in the church's action. Bishop Allen Brown wrote that, "Pewsaction, as an umbrella structure, is committed to the idea that prayer, evangelism, witness, and study are essential things and that responsible Christian action will result just so far as persons have a right relationship with Jesus Christ."[52]

In the middle of the Pewsaction area at the convention was a prayer booth, open during all working hours. Staffed by members of the various Pewsaction fellowships, it offered constant intercession for the work of the convention itself. Many clergy and lay delegates' faith was renewed by visiting that booth for prayer.

It was not anticipated then, but the impact of the Pewsaction coalition was so significant it has had a continuing life ever since. It has become a fellowship of fellowships, and the principal manifestation of its vitality has been the National Episcopal Conferences on Renewal, which have become annual events. Pewsaction has also sponsored a number of

---

*The Conference on the Religious Life in the U.S.A., led by Alfred Pedersen; Fish, led by Philip Deemer; and The Fishermen, led by Gordon Abbott. Since 1973 a number of other groups have joined the coalition.

local and regional conferences, and it was again active at the 1976 General Convention in Minneapolis.

An exciting moment came during the first Renewal Conference in Atlanta in 1974 when the Reverend John Guest, then president of the Fellowship of Witness, announced: *"'We in the Fellowship of Witness are committed to seeing the establishment of a new theological seminary in the Episcopal church, one that is thoroughly biblical and evangelical.''* Thunderous applause swept through the audience, many delegates rising for a lengthy ovation.

Since then the vision has become a reality. On September 26, 1976, Trinity Episcopal School for Ministry held its opening convocation on the Moon Township campus of Robert Morris College, Pittsburgh, Pennsylvania. The renowned missionary statesman, Bishop Alfred Stanway is the new school's first president/dean.

At the opening convocation, Bishop Stanway said, "I remember when we were being trained for the compulsory military training we had in Australia. There was a chap next to me who was waving his gun around wildly. The sergeant-major said, 'Man, if you aim at nothing, you're bound to hit it!' What are you aiming at? Are you like Paul, who said, 'I make it my ambition to please Christ in all things'?"

Pleasing Christ is the great concern of the Renewal Movement generally and of Pewsaction specifically. At the 1976 Renewal Conference, it was announced that a new publishing house and a new church school curriculum were being created for the Episcopal church. Both promise to be thoroughly biblical and evangelical.

And so a pattern seems to be emerging. People encounter new life in Christ in a variety of ways. They discover God's reality out of desperation perhaps. Or they blunder into a charismatic fellowship and have no idea at first what is happening. But they know it is real and they want it. Or perhaps a friend, a member of their family, or their rector receives a spiritual gift or a dramatic answer to prayer and becomes a new person. Perhaps someone explains the basic truths of the gospel in a way they have never heard, and they ask Christ to come into their life. Maybe there is a small Bible study group where they open the Scriptures and embark on a discovery of the greatest story ever told. In one way or another, they get started.

As they go on in their new life in Christ, they wish to ground their experience ever more carefully in truth. They hunger to know the Scriptures, and as they study them, they discover again the great truths of the apostolic age and the Reformation.

Sometimes such people wonder how the Episcopal church moved so far from its origins. Has it lost its Anglican heritage? No, it has merely fallen asleep.

But praise God, it is beginning to wake up—just

as the Israelites did in Ezekiel's day. Ezekiel was a prophet of doom, judgment, and lamentation. His people had been disobedient, and there was no escaping God's punishment. Nevertheless, in the midst of harshness, there was hope.

The Spirit of the Lord led him down into a valley full of dry bones, a very picture of Israel. God asked him, "Son of man, do you think these bones can live?"

"Only you know that, Lord God," he answered.

Then the Lord commanded Ezekiel to prophesy. As he proclaimed the Word of God over the dry bones, the wind began to blow. The wind became breath, the breath became Spirit, and the Spirit touched the dead, dry bones—and they sprang to life again. Flesh and sinews covered them, and they stood upon their feet, "an exceedingly great host" (Ezek. 37:1-10). And the Lord says to the slumbering church, "Wake up, for I will do it again."

Questions for Thought and Discussion

1. What reasons does the author see for the Episcopalian church's loss of membership? Do you agree with these reasons? Can you think of others? Do you agree that the Episcopal church "has majored in the minors"?

2. How do you feel about the renewal movement within the church? Do you feel a need for a more

personal relationship with the Lord?

3. What are the marks that would distinguish the work of God from the efforts of men?

4. What do you think is the key to renewal in the Episcopal church? What can you do about it?

Footnotes

1. Neill, Stephen, *Anglicanism* (London: Penguin, 1958), p. 22.

2. Bainton, Roland, *The Reformation of the Sixteenth Century* (Boston: Beacon, 1952), p. 186.

3. Neill, *Anglicanism*, p. 63.

4. Ryle, J. C., *Five English Reformers* (London: The Banner of Truth Trust, 1960), p. 12.

5. *Ibid.*, p. 30, 31.

6. Foxe, John, *Foxe's Book of Martyrs*, ed. M. G. King (Old Tappan, N.J.: Revell, 1968), p. 192.

7. *Ibid.*, p. 270-272.

8. Loane, Marcus L., *Masters of the English Reformation* (London: The Church Book Room Press, 1954), p. 222.

9. *Ibid.*, p. 237.

10. *Ibid.*, p. 239.

11. *Ibid.*, p. 239.

12. Hooker, Richard, *Of the Laws of Ecclesiastical Polity*, Vol. 1 (London: Everyman's Library, 1907), p. 102.

13. Neill, *Anglicanism*, p. 131, 132.

14. Gray, William and Betty, *The Episcopal Church Welcomes You* (New York: Seabury, 1974), p. 59, 61, [emphasis added].

15. Shepherd, M. H., Jr., *The Oxford American Prayer Book Commentary* (New York: Oxford, 1950), p. 601.

16. Hughes, Philip E., "What About the Thirty-nine Articles?" *Fellowship of Witness Newsletter* (September 1974), p. 1.

17. Shepherd, *The Oxford American Prayer Book Commentary*, p. 601.

18. The Preamble to the Constitution (1973), p. 1.

19. Chorley, E. Clowes, *Men and Movements in the American Episcopal Church* (Hamden: Archon, 1946), p. 39.

20. Goodwin, W. A. R., quoted by Chorley, *Ibid.,* p. 44.

21. McKim, R. H., quoted by Chorley, *Ibid.,* p. 47.

22. Clark, T. H., quoted by Chorley, *Ibid.,* p. 49.

23. Albright, Raymond W., *A History of the Protestant Episcopal Church* (New York: MacMillan, 1964), p. 233.

24. *Ibid.*

25. *Ibid.,* p. 275.

26. Morris, Leon, *Ministers of God* (London: Inter-Varsity, 1964), p. 30, 31.

27. Dix, Gregory, *The Shape of the Liturgy* (London: Dacre, 1945), see chapter two.

28. *Ibid.,* p. 41.

29. Hughes, Philip E., *Theology of the English Reformers* (Grand Rapids: Eerdmans, 1965), p. 152.

30. Dix, *Shape of the Liturgy,* p. 334.

31. Macgregor, G. H. C., "Exegesis, the Acts of the Apostles," *The Interpreter's Bible,* vol. IX (New York: Abingdon, 1954), p. 51.

32. Harnack, Adolph, *History of Dogma,* vol. IV (New York: Dover, 1961), p. 287, 288 [emphasis added].

33. Harnack, *History of Dogma,* vol. 1, p. 211.

34. Walker, Williston, *A History of the Christian Church* (New York: Scribner's, 1959), p. 192.

35. Harnack, *History of Dogma,* vol. V, p. 315.

36. Walker, *History of Christian Church*, p. 239.

37. *Ibid*.

38. Ryle, J. C., *Knots Untied* (London: James Clarke, 1959), p. 138.

39. *Ibid*.

40. *Ibid*.

41. *Ibid*.

42. Walker, *History of Christian Church*, p. 87.

43. Jeremias, Joachim, *The Origins of Infant Baptism* (London: SCM, 1963), p. 22.

44. cf. Jeremias, *Ibid.*, p. 11.

45. Ryle, *Knots Untied*, p. 116.

46. *Ibid*.

47. Hines, John M., *By Water and the Holy Spirit* (New York: Seabury, 1973), p. 76.

48. *Ibid.*, p. 77.

49. Jones, James W., *Filled with New Wine* (New York: Harper and Row, 1974), p. 38, 39.

50. Pulkingham, Graham, *Gathered for Power* (New York: Morehouse-Barlow, 1972), b.c.

51. Stott, John, "World-Wide Evangelical Anglicanism," *Evangelicals Today*, John King, ed. (London: Lutterworth, 1973), p. 177.

52. Brown, Allen W., "Pewsaction," *The Living Church* (reprint, Sept. 9, 1973).